East Timor (Timo Leste)

History, Government and Politics, People, Culture and Religion

Author
Peter Owen

Copyright Notice

Copyright © 2017 Global Print Digital
All Rights Reserved

<u>Digital Management Copyright Notice</u>. This Title is not in public domain, it is copyrighted to the original author, and being published by **Global Print Digital**. No other means of reproducing this title is accepted, and none of its content is editable, neither right to commercialize it is accepted, except with the consent of the author or authorized distributor. You must purchase this Title from a vendor who's right is given to sell it, other sources of purchase are not accepted, and accountable for an action against. We are happy that you understood, and being guided by these terms as you proceed. Thank you

First Printing: 2017.

ISBN: 978-1-912483-02-0

Publisher: Global Print Digital.
Arlington Row, Bibury, Cirencester GL7 5ND
Gloucester
United Kingdom.
Website: www.homeworkoffer.com

Table of Content

Introduction 1
History 3
   Decolonisation, coup, and independence 4
   Indonesian invasion and occupation, with US support 10
   Towards independence 16
   The independent republic 19
   Demographic 20
Politics 24
   Government 24
      Head of State 25
      Head of Government 29
      National Assembley 33
      Ministers 35
      Government Ministries 36
         Structure of the VI Constitutional Government 37
Economy 82
   Oil 89
People and Culture 94
   Literature 94
   Music 95
   Religion 96
      Religion in more Detail 98
         Catholicism and Ancestral Cults 98
         Political activism and role of the Catholic Church in East Timor 112
   Language 116

Introduction

This information book is intended as a general introduction to the people, culture, history and politics of the Democratic Republic of Timor Leste. While specialists might find the bibliography useful to some degree, the book is designed for a more general audience, particularly educators who wish to enhance their social science course content with Southeast Asian material. East Timor is after all the youngest, and perhaps least known, nation of Southeast Asia.

The book is informed by a wide range of literature, historians, as well as on-going ethnographic field research. Certain sections of the book are influenced by these research interests and thus include original field data. The special issues that will be highlighted will focus on some current controversies surrounding: History. People, Culture, Language, Religion. Political activism and role of the Catholic Church in East Timor.

Peter Owen

The book is a single part, that constitutes four principal headings, each of which will provide details related to its heading stated as follow; Introduction, History, Politics, Economy, People and Culture.

History

Portuguese rule

From the 16th century onwards, East Timor was a Portuguese colony known as Portuguese Timor. The rest of the island of Timor, and the other islands that were later to become Indonesia, were colonised by the Dutch between the 17th and 19th centuries, and were known as the Dutch East Indies. Portugal largely neglected the colony, using it mainly as a place to exile those who the government in Lisbon saw as "problems" - these included political prisoners as well as ordinary criminals.

Although Portugal was neutral during World War II, in December 1941, Portuguese Timor was occupied by Australian and Dutch forces, which were expecting a Japanese invasion. When the Japanese did occupy Timor, in February 1942, the Allies and Timorese volunteers engaged them in a guerilla campaign. (See: Battle of Timor (1942-43).) This assistance cost the civilian population dearly: Japanese forces burned many villages and seized food supplies. The Japanese occupation resulted in the deaths of 40,000-70,000 Timorese.

Portuguese Timor was handed back to Portugal after the war, but Portugal continued to neglect the colony. Very little investment was made in infrastructure, education and healthcare. The colony was declared an 'Overseas Province' of the Portuguese Republic in 1955. Locally, authority rested with the Portuguese Governor and the Legislative Council, as well as local chiefs or liurai. Only a small minority of Timorese were educated, and even fewer went on to university in Portugal.

During this time, Indonesia did not express any interest in Portuguese Timor, despite the anti-colonial rhetoric of President Sukarno. This was partly as Indonesia was preoccupied with gaining control of West Irian in New Guinea, which had been retained by the Netherlands after Indonesian independence. In fact, at the United Nations, Indonesian diplomats stressed that their country did not seek control over any territory outside the former Netherlands East Indies, explicitly mentioning Portuguese Timor.

Decolonisation, coup, and independence

After the fall of the Portuguese fascist regime in 1974, independence was encouraged by the new, democratic Portuguese government.

One of the first acts of the new government in Lisbon was to appoint a new Governor for the colony on November 18, 1974, in the form of Mário Lemos Pires, who would ultimately be, as events were to prove, the last Governor of Portuguese Timor.

One of his first decrees made upon his arrival in Dili was to legalise political parties in preparation for elections to a Constituent Assembly in 1976. Three main political parties were formed:

The União Democrática Timorense (Timorese Democratic Union or UDT), was supported by the traditional elites, initially supported continued association with Lisbon, or as they put it in Tetum, mate bandera hum - 'in the shadow of the [Portuguese] flag', but later adopted a 'gradualist' approach to independence. One of its leaders, Mario Viegas Carrascalão, one of the few Timorese to have been educated at university in Portugal, later became Indonesian Governor of East Timor during the 1980s and early 1990s, although with the demise of Indonesian rule, he would change to supporting independence.

The Associação Social Democrática Timorese (Timorese Social Democratic Association ASDT) supported a rapid movement to independence. It later changed its name to Frente Revolucionaria de Timor Leste Independente (Revolutionary Front of Independent East Timor or Fretilin). Fretilin was criticised by many in Australia and Indonesia as being Marxist, its name sounding reminiscent of FRELIMO in Mozambique but it was more influenced by African nationalists like Amílcar Cabral in Portuguese Guinea (now Guinea-Bissau) and Cape Verde.

The Associação Popular Democrática Timorese (Timorese Popular Democratic Association or Apodeti) supported integration with Indonesia, as an autonomous province, but had very little grassroots support. One of its leaders, Abilio Osorio Soares, later served as the last Indonesian-appointed Governor of East Timor. Apodeti drew support from a few liurai in the border region, some of whom had collaborated with the Japanese during the Second World War. It also had some support in the small Muslim minority, although Marí Alkatiri, a Muslim, was a prominent Fretilin leader, and became Prime Minister in 2002.

Other smaller parties included Klibur Oan Timur Asuwain or KOTA whose name translated from the Tetum language as 'Sons of the Mountain Warriors', which sought to create a form of monarchy involving the local liurai, and the Partido Trabalhista or Labour Party, but neither had any significant support. They would, however, collaborate with Indonesia. The Associação Democratica para a Integração de Timor Leste na Austrália (ADITLA), advocated integration with Australia, but folded after the Australian government emphatically ruled out the idea.

Developments in Portuguese Timor during 1974 and 1975 were watched closely by Indonesia and Australia. The Suharto regime, which had ruthlessly suppressed Indonesia's Communist Party PKI in 1965, was alarmed by what it saw as the increasingly left-leaning Fretilin, and by the prospect of a small state in the midst of the sprawling archipelago serving as an inspiration to independence-minded provinces of the Republic such as Aceh, West Irian and the Moluccas.

Australia's Labor Prime Minister, Gough Whitlam, had developed a close working relationship with the Indonesian leader, and also followed events with concern. At a meeting in the Javanese town of Wonosobo in 1974, he told Suharto that an independent Timor would be 'an unviable state, and a potential threat to the stability of the region'. While recognising the need for an act of self-determination, he considered integration with Indonesia to be in Timor's best interests.

In local elections on 13th March 1975, Fretilin and UDT emerged as the largest parties, having previously formed an alliance to campaign for independence. Indonesian military intelligence, known as BAKIN, began attempting to cause divisions between the pro-independence parties, and promote the support of Apodeti. This was known as Operasi Komodo or 'Operation Komodo' after the giant Komodo lizard found in the eastern Indonesian island of the same name. Many Indonesian military figures held meetings with UDT leaders, who made it plain that Jakarta would not tolerate a Fretilin-led administration in an independent East Timor. The coalition between Fretilin and UDT later broke up.

During the course of 1975, Portugal became increasingly detached from political developments in its colony, becoming embroiled in civil unrest and political crises, and more concerned with decolonisation in its African colonies of Angola and Mozambique than with Portuguese Timor. Many local leaders saw independence as unrealistic, and were open to discussions with Jakarta over Portuguese Timor's incorporation into the Indonesian state.

The United States had also expressed concerns over Portuguese Timor in the wake of the war in Vietnam. Having gained Indonesia as an ally,

Washington did not want to see the vast archipelago destabilised by a left-wing regime in its midst.

On August 11, 1975, the UDT mounted a coup, in a bid to halt the increasing popularity of Fretilin. Governor Pires fled to the offshore island of Atauro, north of the capital, Dili, from where he later attempted to broker an agreement between the two sides. He was urged by Fretilin to return and resume the decolonisation process, but he insisted that he was awaiting instructions from the government in Lisbon, now increasingly uninterested.

Indonesia sought to portray the conflict as a civil war, which had plunged Portuguese Timor into anarchy and chaos, but after only a month, aid and relief agencies from Australia and elsewhere visited the territory, and reported that the situation was stable. Nevertheless, many UDT supporters had fled across the border into Indonesian Timor, where they were coerced into supporting integration with Indonesia. In October 1975, in the border town of Balibo, two Australian television crews reporting on the conflict were killed by Indonesian forces, after they witnessed Indonesian incursions into Portuguese Timor.

While Fretilin had sought the return of the Portuguese Governor, pointedly flying the Portuguese flag from government offices, the deteriorating situation meant that it had to make an appeal to the world for international support, independently of Portugal.

On November 28, 1975, Fretilin made a unilateral declaration of independence of the Democratic Republic of East Timor (Republica Democrática de Timor Leste in Portuguese). This was not recognised by either Portugal, Indonesia, or Australia. Fretilin's Francisco Xavier do Amaral became the first President, while Fretilin leader Nicolau dos Reis Lobato was Prime Minister. Indonesia's response was to have UDT, Apodeti, KOTA and Trabalhista leaders sign a declaration calling for integration with Indonesia called the Balibo Declaration, although it was drafted by Indonesian intelligence and signed in Bali, Indonesia not Balibo, Portuguese Timor. Xanana Gusmão, now the country's President, described this as the 'Balibohong Declaration', a pun on the Indonesian word for 'lie'.

Indonesian invasion and occupation, with US support

On December 7, Indonesian forces launched a massive air and sea invasion, known as Operasi Seroja, or 'Operation Lotus', almost entirely using US supplied equipment.

A year earlier, in December 1974, Henry Kissinger of the US government had been asked by an Indonesian government representative whether or not the US would approve the invasion. In March 1975, US Ambassador to Indonesia, David Newsom, recommended a policy of silence on the issue and was supported by Kissinger. On October 8, 1974, a member of the National Security Council, Philip Habib, told meeting participants that It looks like the Indonesians have begun the attack on Timor. Kissinger's response to his staff was to ask, I'm assuming you're really going to keep your mouth shut on this subject?

On the day before the invasion, US President Gerald Ford and Henry Kissinger met with Indonesia's Suharto. According to declassified documents released by the National Security Archive (NSA), in December of 2001, they gave a green light for the invasion. In response to Suharto saying "We want your understanding if it was deemed necessary to take rapid or drastic action [in East Timor]." Ford replied, "We will understand and not press you on the issue. We understand the problem and the intentions you have." Kissinger similarly agreed, though he had fears that the use of US-made arms in the invasion would be exposed to public scrutiny, talking of their desire to "influence the reaction in America" so that "there would be less chance of people talking in an unauthorised way".

Similarly, Australian governments protested loudly in public after the event but had already provided private assurances that no substantive action would be taken. This was an unpopular policy with the Australian public, as the heroic actions of the Timorese people during World War II were well-remembered, and vigorous protests took place in Australia, but to no avail. It is widely believed that the primary motivating factor for the Whitlam and Fraser governments lack of opposition was the possibility of oil being found in the waters between Australia and Timor.

During the invasion mass killings and rapes took place: 60,000 Timorese were dead by mid-February. A puppet Provisional Government of East Timor was installed in mid-December, consisting of Apodeti and UDT leaders. Attempts by the United Nations Secretary General's Special Representative, Vittorio Winspeare Guicciardi to visit Fretilin-held areas from Darwin, Australia were obstructed by the Indonesian military, which blockaded East Timor. On May 31, 1976, a 'People's Assembly' in Dili, selected by Indonesian intelligence, unanimously endorsed an 'Act of Integration', and on July 17, East Timor officially became the 27th province of the Republic of Indonesia. Although the United Nations had turned a blind eye to the Indonesian annexation of West Irian some years previously, the occupation of East Timor remained a public issue in many nations, Portugal in particular, and the UN never recognised either the regime installed by the Indonesians or the subsequent annexation.

In fact on December 12, 1975, the United Nations General Assembly approved a resolution according to which, "having heard the statements of the representatives of Portugal, as the Administering Power, concerning developments in Portuguese Timor...deplores the military intervention of the armed forces of Indonesia in Portuguese Timor and calls upon the Government of Indonesia to withdraw without delay its armed forces from the Territory...and recommends that the Security Council take urgent action to protect the territorial integrity of Portuguese Timor and the inalienable right of its people to self-determination".

However, Daniel Patrick Moynihan, the US ambassador to the UN at the time, wrote in his biography that "the United States wished things to turn out as they did, and worked to bring this about. The Department of State desired that the United Nations prove utterly ineffective in whatever measures it undertook [with regard to the invasion of East Timor]. This task was given to me, and I carried it forward with not inconsiderable success." (A Dangerous Place, Little Brown, 1980, p. 247) Later, he admitted that as American ambassador to the UN, he had defended a "shameless" Cold War policy toward East Timor.

Western governments were criticized during the war for their role in supporting the Indonesian government, for example with arms sales. The U.S. had supported Suharto's regime in Indonesia during the Cold War as it was seen as a bulwark against communism and it continued the practice during the invasion of East Timor. While the U.S. government claimed to have suspended military assistance from December 1975 to June 1976, military aid was actually above what the Department of State proposed and Congress continued to increase it.

The U.S. also made four new offers of arms, including supplies and parts for OV-10 Broncos which, according to Cornell University Professor Benedict Anderson, are "specially designed for counter-insurgency actions against adversaries without effective anti-aircraft weapons and wholly useless for defending Indonesia against a foreign enemy", adding that the policy continued under the Carter administration.

Testifying before Congress, the Deputy Legal Advisor of the State Department, George Aldrich aid the Indonesians "were armed roughly 90 percent with our equipment. ... we really did not know very much. Maybe we did not want to know very much but I gather that for a time we did not know." Indonesia was never informed of the supposed US "aid suspension". David T. Kenney, Country Officer for Indonesia in the State Department, also testified before Congress that one purpose for the arms was "to keep that area [Timor] peaceful.

"The invasion was not given much coverage by the U.S. media. When the subject was covered, the deaths were attributed to the preceding civil war. This caused some to later accuse the media of blatant bias, because coverage of the genocide in Cambodia under the Khmer Rouge was much more common.

In 1992 the United States ended its military training programme in Indonesia, and in 1994 the United States banned the export of small arms and riot control equipment to that country. Nevertheless, organisations monitoring trade in arms have estimated that between 1992 and 1997 the United States sold more than $1 billion worth of arms to Indonesia. In 1995 the training programme was resumed but included lessons about human rights and the control of civilian crowds. The Joint Combined Exchange Training program managed by Green Berets and Air Force commandos continued until 1996 without the knowledge of Congress. The fact that some of the aircraft sold to the Indonesian army were not designed for offensive purposes did not prevent them from being so used. Arms sales to Indonesia remained suspended until a promise was received that lethal weapons and helicopters would not be used in East Timor. The UK government is also known to have allowed the sales of arms to be used in East Timor.

Towards independence

Several Timorese groups fought a resistance war against Indonesian forces for the independence of East Timor, during which many atrocities and human rights violations by the Indonesian army were reported. A sad highpoint was the killing of many East Timorese youngsters (reportedly over 250) at a cemetery in Dili on November 12, 1991. In total, estimates of the number of deaths in the war range from 100,000 to 200,000—out of a total East Timorese population of only 800,000.

The Dili Massacre was to prove the turning point for sympathy to the East Timorese cause in the world arena as, with the dissolution of the Soviet Union that same year, the "Marxist bogey" that Indonesia had often used against the idea of an independent East Timor had vanished.

The Massacre had a profound effect on public opinion in Portugal, especially after television footage showing East Timorese praying in Portuguese, and independence leader Xanana Gusmão gained widespread respect, being awarded the Portugal's highest honour in 1993, after he had been captured and imprisoned by the Indonesians.

In Australia, there was also widespread public outrage, and criticism of Canberra's close relationship with the Suharto regime and recognition of Jakarta's sovereignty over East Timor. This caused the Australian government embarrassment, but Foreign Minister Gareth Evans played down the killings, describing them as 'an aberration, not an act of state policy'.

Portugal started to apply international pressure unsuccessfully, constantly raising the issue with its fellow European Union members in their dealings with Indonesia. However, other EU countries like the UK had close economic relations with Indonesia, including arms sales, and saw no advantage in forcefully raising the issue.

In 1996, Bishop Carlos Felipe Ximenes Belo and Jose Ramos-Horta, two leading East Timorese activists for peace and independence, received the Nobel Peace Prize.

In 1998, following the resignation of Suharto and his replacement by President Habibie, Jakarta moved towards offering East Timor autonomy within the Indonesian state, although ruled out independence, and stated that Portugal and the UN must recognise Indonesian sovereignty.

However in 1999, the Indonesian government decided, under strong international pressure, to hold a referendum about the future of East Timor. Portugal had started to gain some political allies firstly in the EU, and after that in other places of the world to pressure Indonesia. The referendum, held on August 30, gave a clear majority (78.5%) in favour of independence, rejecting the alternative offer of being an autonomous province within Indonesia, to be known as the Special Autonomous Region of East Timor (SARET).Directly after this, Indonesian-backed paramilitaries as well as Indonesian soldiers carried out a campaign of violence and terrorism in retaliation. According to Noam Chomsky, "In one month, this massive military operation murdered some 2,000 people, raped hundreds of women and girls, displaced three-quarters of the population, and demolished 75 percent of the country's infrastructure" (Radical Priorities, 72).

Activists in Portugal, Australia, the United States, and elsewhere pressured their governments to take action, with US President Bill Clinton eventually threatening Indonesia, in dire economic straits already, with the withdrawal of IMF loans. The Indonesian government consented to withdraw its troops and allow a multinational force into Timor to stablilize the area.

It was clear that the UN did not have sufficient resources to combat the paramilitary forces directly. Instead, the UN authorised the creation of a multinational military force known as INTERFET (International Force for East Timor), with Security Council Resolution 1264. Troops were contributed by 17 nations, about 9,900 in total. 4,400 came from Australia, the remainder mostly from South-East Asia [6]. The force was led by Major-General (now General) Peter Cosgrove. Troops landed in East Timor on September 20, 1999.

The independent republic

The administration of East Timor was taken over by the UN through the United Nations Transitional Administration for East Timor (UNTAET), established on October 25 [7]. The INTERFET deployment ended on February 14, 2000 with the transfer of military command to the UN [8]. Elections were held in late 2001 for a constituent assembly to draft a constitution, a task finished in February 2002. East Timor became formally independent on May 20, 2002. Xanana Gusmão was sworn in as the country's President. East Timor became a member of the UN on September 27, 2002.

On December 4, 2002, after a student had been arrested the previous day, rioting students set fire to the house of the Prime Minister Marí Alkatiri and advanced on the police station. The police opened fire and one student was killed, whose body the students carried to the National Parliament building. There they fought the police, set a supermarket on fire and plundered shops. The police opened fire again and four more students were killed. Alkatiri called an inquiry and blamed foreign influence for the violence.

Relations with Australia have been strained by disputes over the maritime boundary between the two countries. Canberra claims petroleum and natural gas fields in an area known as the 'Timor Gap', which East Timor regards as lying within its maritime boundaries.

Demographic

The Timorese are known collectively as Maubere, an originally derogatory name turned into a name of pride by the resistance movement. Timorese consist of a number of distinct ethnic groups, most of whom are of mixed Malayo-Polynesian descent and Melanesian/Papuan stock.

The largest Malayo-Polynesian ethnic groups are the Tetun (or Tetum) (100,000), primarily living in the north coast and around Dili, the Mambae (80,000), living in the mountains of central East Timor, the Tukudede (63,170), who are living in the area around Maubara and Liquisa, the Galoli (50,000) living between the tribes of Mambae and

Makasae, Kemak (50,000) in north-central Timor island, and the Baikeno (20,000), living in the area around Pantemakassar.

The main tribes of predominantly Papuan origin include the Bunak (50,000) living in Central interior Timor island, the Fataluku (30,000) living in the eastern tip of East Timor around Los Palos, and the Makasae living in the eastern end of the island.

The Timorese are a racially mixed people composed of Melanesian and Malay genetic elements. In addition, in common with other former Portuguese colonies where interracial marriage was common, there is also smaller population of people of mixed Timorese and Portuguese origin, known in Portuguese as Mestiço. The best-known East Timorese Mestiço internationally is José Ramos Horta, spokesman for the resistance movement in exile, now Foreign Minister. Mário Viegas Carrascalão, Indonesia's appointed governor between 1987 and 1992, is also Mestiço.

The population is predominantly Roman Catholic (90%), with sizable Muslim (5%) and Protestant (3%) minorities. Smaller Hindu, Buddhist and animist minorities make up the remainder. Currently, there are about a million citizens of East Timor.

Population: 952,618 (July 2002 est.)
note: other estimates range as low as 800,000 (2002 est.)

Population growth rate: 7.26% (2002 est.)

Birth rate: 28.07 births/1,000 population (2002 est.)

Death rate: 6.52 deaths/1,000 population (2002 est.)

Net migration rate: 51.07 migrant(s)/1,000 population (2002 est.)

Infant mortality rate: 51.99 deaths/1,000 live births (2002 est.)

Life expectancy at birth:
total population: 64.85 years
male: 62.64 years
female: 67.17 years (2002 est.)

Total fertility rate: 3.88 children born/woman (2002 est.)

Nationality:
noun: Timorese
adjective: Timorese

Ethnic groups: Austronesian (Malayo-Polynesian), Papuan, small Chinese minority

Religions: Roman Catholic 90%, Muslim 4%, Protestant 3%, Hindu 0.5%, Buddhist, Animist (1992 est.) The Timorese government reports[1] that most Christians continue to practice animist traditions. A minority, called Serani, do not.

Languages: Tetum (official), Portuguese (official), Bahasa Indonesia, English

note: there are a total of about 16 indigenous languages, of which Tetum, Galole, Mambae, and Kemak are spoken by significant numbers of people

Literacy:

definition: age 15 and over can read and write

total population: 48% (2001)

Politics

Government

The Head of state of the East Timorese republic is the president, who is elected by popular vote for a five-year term and whose role is largely symbolic, though he is able to veto some legislation. Following elections, the president appoints as prime minister the leader of the majority party or majority coalition. As head of government the prime minister presides over the Council of State or cabinet.

The unicameral Timorese parliament is the National Parliament or Parlamento Nacional, whose members are elected by popular vote to a five-year term. The number of seats can vary from a minimum of 52 to a maximum of 65, though it exceptionally has 88 members at present, due to this being its first term of office. The Timorese constitution was modelled on that of Portugal. The country is still in the process of building its administration and governmental institutions.

- ➢ **Head of State**
- ➢ **Head of Government**
- ➢ **National Assembly**
- ➢ **Ministers**
- ➢ **Government Departments**

Head of State

East Timor's constitution took effect when the territory officially became independent in May 2002. It provides for a democratic republic with a president as head of state and a prime minister as head of government. All citizens aged 18 and older have the right to vote.

The president of East Timor is directly elected to serve a five-year term and may serve no more than two consecutive terms. Under the constitution, the president is the symbol of East Timorese independence and the guarantor of the smooth functioning of the republic's democratic institutions. The president is the supreme commander of the defense forces.

Kay Rala Xanana Gusmão (born June 20, 1946), born José Alexandre Gusmão, is the inaugural President of the small nation of East Timor in Southeast Asia.

Gusmão was born to school-teacher parents in Manaututo in what was then Portuguese Timor, and attended a Jesuit high school just outside of Dili. After leaving high-school at the age of sixteen (for financial reasons), he worked a variety of unskilled jobs, although he continued his education at evening college. In 1965, at the age of 19, he met Emilia Batista, who was later to become his wife.

In 1966 Gusmão obtained a position with the public service, which allowed him to continue his education. This was interrupted in 1968 when Gusmão was recruited in the Portuguese army for national service.

He served for three years, rising to the rank of corporal. During this time he married Emilia Batista, by whom he had two children, his son Eugenio, and daughter Zenilda.

He relates that his people told him to 'never give up' and he found himself in having to rebuild the shattered resistance

1971 was a turning point for Gusmão. He completed his national service, his son was born, and he became involved with a nationalist organisation headed by José Ramos Horta. For the next three years he was actively involved in peaceful protests at the colonial system.

It was in 1974 that a left-wing coup in Portugal resulted in the beginning of decolonisation for Portuguese Timor, and shortly afterwards the Governor Mário Lemos Pires announced plans to grant the colony independence. Plans were drawn up to hold general elections with a view to independence in 1978.

During most of 1975 a bitter internal struggle occurred between two rival factions in Portuguese Timor. Gusmão became deeply involved with the Fretilin faction, and as a result he was arrested and imprisoned by the rival faction the Timorese Democratic Union (UDT) in mid-1975.

Taking advantage of the internal disorder, and with an eye to absorbing the colony, Indonesia immediately began a campaign of destabilisation, and frequent raids into Portuguese Timor were staged from Indonesian Timor.

By late 1975 the Fretilin faction had gained control of Portuguese Timor and Gusmão was released. He was given the position of Press Secretary within the Fretilin organisation. On November 28, 1975, Fretilin declared the independence of Portuguese Timor as "The

Democratic Republic of East Timor", and Gusmão was responsible for filming the ceremony.

Nine days later Indonesia invaded East Timor. At the time Gusmão was visiting friends outside of Dili and he witnessed the invasion from the hills. For the next few days he searched for his family.

During the early 1990s Gusmão became heavily involved in diplomacy and media management, and was instrumental in alerting the world to the massacre that occurred in Santa Cruz on November 12, 1991. Gusmão was interviewed by many major media channels and obtained worldwide attention.

As a result of his high profile, Gusmão became a prime target of the Indonesian government. A campaign for his capture was finally successful in November 1992. In May, 1993, Gusmão was tried, convicted and sentenced to life imprisonment by the Indonesian Government. He was denied the right to a defence. Although not released until late 1999, Gusmão successfully led the resistance from within prison. During this time he was regularly visited by United Nations representatives, and dignitaries such as Nelson Mandela.

The man who had led the East Timorese through fratricide, occupation and the independence ballot, had finally agreed to run as the new nation's first head of state

On August 30, 1999, a referendum was held in East Timor and an overwhelming majority voted for independence. The Indonesian military commenced a campaign of terror as a result, with terrible consequences. Although the Indonesian government denied ordering this offensive, they were widely condemned for failing to prevent it. As a result of overwhelming diplomatic pressure from the United Nations, and particularly the United States and Australia, an Australian-led UN-peacekeeping force entered East Timor, and Gusmão was finally released. Upon his return to Dili, he began a campaign of reconciliation and rebuilding.

Gusmão was appointed to a senior role in the UN administration that governed East Timor until 2002. During this time he continually campaigned for unity and peace within East Timor, and was generally regarded as the de facto leader of the emerging nation. Elections were held in late 2001 and Gusmão was comfortably elected leader. As a result he became the first President of East Timor when it became formally independent on May 20, 2002.

Head of Government

East Timor's constitution took effect when the territory officially became independent inMay 2002. It provides for a democratic republic with a president as head of state and a prime minister as head of government. All citizens aged 18 and older have the right to vote.

The prime minister oversees the day-to-day functioning of government and chairs the Council of Ministers. The prime minister is designated by the political party or alliance of political parties with a majority in the national legislature and formally appointed by the president. Ministers are also appointed by the president, following the recommendations of the prime minister.

As head of the first government of an independent Timor-Leste, the Prime Minister is charged with the enormous task of building a government from almost nothing. The United Nations second mission in Timor-Leste (UNTAET - United Nations Transitional Administration East Timor) acted as the governing body of Timor-Leste from 2000 to May 20, 2002 when Timor-Leste made the final transition to independence.

Now, the Prime Minister and his government are rebuilding the country and its institutions with minimal resources including a severe lack of human resources and skills. They are reconstructing a nation in which most homes, government buildings and essential infrastructure were destroyed by exiting Indonesian militia in 1999 after an overwhelming vote for independence. The government is facing the challenges of unacceptably high rates of illiteracy, infant mortality, and post-conflict trauma. Most people in Timor-Leste do not have access to running water or electricity in their homes. And, the people of Timor-Leste are coming to terms with freedom and the ideals of democracy after more than 400 years of colonization and occupation.

This first government of Timor-Leste and its Prime Minister Mari Alkatiri, have tackled these difficulties in the first two years of its five year term. With the support of its development partners, the government has written and approved the Timor-Leste Constitution, and in accordance with the Constitution a National Development Plan and The Road Map for the implementation of NDP programs. The Timor-Leste Government is considered by the World Bank to be the 'strongest institution in Timor-Leste". Despite weaknesses in other institutions the government upholds and practices the principles of transparency, accountability and the rule of law.

The Prime Minister is committed to ensuring the government continues to reduce poverty and improve the livelihoods of the people of Timor-Leste. He is also committed to ensuring the development of all important sectors relevant to this objective as set out in the National Development Plan with the hope of a prosperous and safe future for Timor-Leste.

While East Timor's President, Xanana Gusmao -a former guerrilla fighter and poet - is viewed as a charismatic "man of the people", Prime Minister Mari Alkatiri is lower profile and is seen as more elusive. Alkatiri helped to found the independence party Fretilin.

Marí bim Amude Alkatiri (born 26 November 1949) is the first Prime Minister of an internationally recognized East Timor. Before entering politics, he was a chartered surveyor, and lived in exile during Indonesian occupation.The 54-year-old former chartered surveyor spent the years of Indonesia's occupation of East Timor living in political exile, only returning to the territory in 1999 ahead of the vote for independence. He was engaged in academic teaching in Mozambique.

But he established his political roots from an early age.

He entered political life in January 1970, when he was 20, with the establishment of the Movement for the Liberation of East Timor when the territory was still under Portuguese rule.

Mr Alkatiri went on to become one of the founder members of Fretilin, the party which was instrumental in achieving East Timor's independence from Indonesian rule.

When East Timor finally voted to become independent he entered the interim administration as economics minister, forging his reputation as a tough operator as chief negotiator over the rich petroleum resources in the sea between Australia and Timor.

The Prime Minister is the head of the Timor-Leste Government and is ultimately responsible to the people of Timor-Leste for policy development and the decisions taken by the government.

National Assembley

Politics: Unicameral Parliamentry System

Head of state of the East Timorese republic is the president, who is elected by popular vote for a five-year term and whose role is largely symbolic, though he is able to veto some legislation. Following legislative elections, the president appoints as prime minister the leader of the majority party or majority coalition. As head of government the prime minister presides over the Council of State or cabinet.

The unicameral Timorese parliament is the National Parliament or Parlamento Nacional, whose members are also elected by popular vote to a five-year term. The number of seats can vary from a minimum of 52 to a maximum of 65, though it exceptionally has 88 members at present, due to this being its first term of office. The

Timorese constitution was modelled on that of Portugal. The country is still in the process of building its administration and governmental institutions.

The National Parliament consists of 88 members who were elected on 30 August 2001 to the Constituent Assembly. The Constituent Assembly's directive was to develop a Constitution for East Timor. With the approval of the Constitution, the Constituent Assembly has been transformed into a National Parliament for up to five years. The National Parliament will be responsible for making laws on issues concerning the country's domestic and foreign policy, as well as other functions set out in the Constitution. Specific objectives of the National Parliament are as follows:

- Pass relevant, well drafted legislation in a timely manner;
- Establish a multiparty system and democratic rules through a productive dialogue;
- Provide a counterbalance to the powers of the Presidency and of the Government; and
- Establish and maintain proper, efficient and effective communication between the various branches of the Government in order to ensure respect for the Constitution and

constitutionally enacted laws, transparency within the public administration, and the independence and impartiality of the judiciary.

The Parliament function is supported by the Secretariat that it may provides right services to the Members. The services of the Secretariat include the list of the deliberations of the Parliament and the administration on the legislative agenda.

Ministers

Marí bim Amude Alkatiri is the first Prime Minister of an internationally recognized Timor-Leste. Before entering politics, he was a chartered surveyor, and lived in exile during Indonesian occupation.

As the Chief of Government, he is supported by the Minister in the Presidency of the Council of Ministers and by the Secretary of State for Parliamentary Affairs. The following services and bodies are directly under the Prime Minister. He is also responsible for those that are not formally integrated in a Ministry or Secretariat of State such as the Timor Sea Office and the Government Information Office:

- ➢ National Service for State Security
- ➢ Inspector-General

- Office of the Advisor for Human Rights
- Office of the Advisor for Image and Social Communications
- Office of the Advisor of Promotion of Equality
- Capacity Development Coordination Unit
- The Banking and Payments Authority

The Prime Minister is responsible for the defence and implementation of budget statements and government policy generally. Although he consults widely and must seek the approval from the Council of Ministers, he is ultimately responsible for all government decisions.

Government Ministries

Ministry of Foreign Affairs & Cooperation

Ministry of Internal Affairs

Ministry of Justice

Ministry of Agriculture, Forestry and Fisheries

Ministry of Health

Ministry of Transport & Communication

Ministry of Education & Culture

Ministry of Planning & Finance

Ministry of Development

Ministry of Internal Administration

Ministry of Public Works

Ministry of the Labor and Solidarity

Ministry of Defense

Structure of the VI Constitutional Government

1.Prime Minister

Dr. Rui Maria de Araújo

The Prime Minister has its own competence and that delegated by the Council of Ministers, under the Constitution and the Law.

It is especially incumbent upon the Prime Minister, to lead the Government and to preside over the Council of Ministers; to direct and guide overall policy of the Government and the governing action; represent the Government and the Council of Ministers in their relationship with the President of the Republic and the National Parliament; to guide the overall policy of the Government in its external relations and represent the Government regarding the international community; to lead the overall policy of the Government towards CPLP and ASEAN; to direct and guide the overall policy of the Government concerning defence and security and national intelligence; to coordinate the National Security Integrated System; to lead the overall policy of the Government concerning financial management, which includes bank sector, revenue sector and investment of the Petroleum Fund; to appoint a lawyer, according to the law, to represent the State, in case of judicial disputes where the State takes part; to manage the information technology system of the Government and ensure the provision of the concerning services, as well as implement IT systems in the national territory; to coordinate with the Authority for the Special Administrative Region of Oe-cusse Ambeno the administrative autonomy of the Region.

While head of Government, the Prime Minister has the power to issue instructions to any member of Government and to make decisions on subjects included in the areas of the responsibility of any Ministry or Secretariat of State, as well as to create permanent or temporary committees or workgroups for subjects under the Government.

The Prime Minister also has powers regarding the services, bodies and activities under the Presidency of the Council of Ministers that are not the responsibility of the other members of Government that are part of it, and may delegate this power on any member of Government as well as others legally given to him.

The following services and organisms are under the direct purview of the Prime Minister: National Intelligence Service, Council for Permanent Delimitation of Sea Boundaries, Civil Service Commission,

AMRT Archive and Museum of the Timorese Resistance, E-government ITC and the Supporting Office to the Civil Society.

The Prime Minister is assisted by the Minister of State and of the Presidency of the Council of Ministers; the Minister of State and Coordinator of Social Affairs; the Minister of State and Coordinator of Economic Affairs and the Minister of State and Coordinator of State Administration Affairs and Justice.

2. Minister of State and of the Presidency of the Council of Ministers
Agio Pereira

The Minister of State and of the Presidency of the Council of Ministers assists the Prime Minister with the Presidency of the Council of Ministers and with the Government coordination, being the Government spokesperson.

It is primarily up to the Minister of State and of the Presidency of the Council of Ministers to coordinate the preparation and organisation of governmental work, as well as the follow-up and assessment of the decisions taken by the Council of Ministers and the Prime Minister; to coordinate the work meetings of the different Ministers of State and Coordinators of the concerning areas with the Prime Minister for joint assessment of the performance by several Government bodies; to coordinate and implement the reforms to governmental bodies, according to the decisions taken by the Council of Ministers and the Prime Minister; to coordinate the reform of the judicial sector; and to coordinate the legal consultation and support to the Council of Ministers, Prime Minister, Ministers of State and remaining members of Government inside the Presidency of the Council of Ministers.

In addition to the tasks referred to in the preceding paragraph and the ones delegated by the Council of Ministers and the Prime Minister, the Minister of State and of the Presidency of the Council of Ministers also shall: coordinate and centralize the legislative and regulating procedure by the Government; proceed with a thorough study of legal reform, in terms of formal requirements, of standardization and harmonization, as well as in assessing the needs of governmental intervention or from the National Parliament.

Promote a modern legislative procedure, through the use of e-government tools, the disclosure of actions and measures of the Government and organizing the form and means of its public intervention; analyse and prepare the legal and regulatory drafts of the Government, in coordination with the proposing ministries; ensure litigation services for the Presidency of the Council of Ministers; Coordinate the legal representatives of the State, in judicial disputes where the State takes part; reply, in collaboration with the concerning ministry, to procedures aiming to verify constitutionality and legality; assure regular coordination with the National Parliament; translate or follow the translation of legal drafts or other documents needed by the Council of Ministers or the Prime Minister; represent the Council of Ministers and the Prime Minister, whenever decided by them, in specially formed committees; propose the policy and draft the legislation needed for the media sector; Monitor the State media bodies; coordinate the dissemination of information on programs and actions of the Government; and act as spokesperson for the Council of Ministers.

It is also incumbent upon the Minister of State and of the Presidency of the Council of Ministers the supervision of the Secretary of State for the Council of Ministers, of the Secretary of State for Parliamentary Affairs and of the Secretary of State for Media.

It is also upon him the supervision of the RTTL Radio and Television of Timor-Leste, PE and the National Printing.

3. Minister of State, Coordinator of Social Affairs and Minister of Education
António da Conceição

The Minister of State and Coordinator of Social Affairs assists the Prime Minister with the supervision of the general policy for the governance of social affairs, being specifically responsible for the work and activities developed by the Ministry of Education, as the Minister, and Ministry of Health, the Ministry of Social Solidarity, the Secretary of State for Woman Support and Socio-economic Promotion, the Secretary of State for Youth and Sports, the Committee on the Rights of the Child, the National Liberation Fighters and the Commission for Combating HIV/AIDS.

It is primarily up to the Minister of State and Coordinator of Social Affairs to coordinate the preparation and organisation of governmental work for the social field; to follow-up and assess the works and services provided by the Ministry of Health; Ministry of Social Solidarity; Secretary of State for Woman Support and Socio-economic Promotion; Secretary of State for Youth and Sports; Committee on the Rights of the Child; National Liberation Fighters; and the Commission for combating HIV/AIDS; to propose and develop public policies in social areas that account for a better provision of services to the citizens; and to uphold the coordination with relevant entities for social development.

The Minister of State and Coordinator of Social Affairs superintends the Sports National Commission (CND) and the Regulatory Commission for Martial Arts (CRAM).

As the Minister of Education he has competencies to propose and ensure the policy regarding pre-school and school education, comprising basic and secondary education and including special needs education, promoting recurrent education and life-long learning; to take part in the definition and execution of policies regarding qualification and vocational training; to uphold the right to education and assure compulsory education, in order to promote inclusion and equal opportunities; to enforce teaching and learning conditions, adding to the qualification of people and to higher educational attainment and employment; to define the national curricula for the various degrees of education and the assessment regime for students and approve the teaching programs, along with guidelines for its execution; to promote and manage the development and renovation of non-higher education public schools, as well as support any initiatives related with private and co-operative schools; to design policies for higher education, science and technology, including the concerning organization, financing, execution and assessment; to promote equal opportunities of access to higher education; to promote the development, upgrading, quality, competitiveness and international recognition of higher education, scientific and technologic systems; to foster the liaison between higher education, scientific and technologic institutions and between them and the manufacturing system; to raise the permanent assessment and inspection of higher education, scientific and technologic institutions; to foster the assessment of education professionals; and to plan a supervision and analysis system, to assess the results and impacts of education and training policies.

The National University Timor Lorosa'e, the National Institute of Science and Technology, the National Committee of UNESCO, the National Institute for Training of Teachers and Education Professionals (INFORDEPE) and the National Agency for Academic Assessment and Accreditation (ANAAA), are under the supervision of the Minister of Education.

The Ministry of Education is the central Government body responsible for the design, execution, coordination and assessment of the policy defined and approved by the Council of Ministers for the areas of education and qualification, as well as science and technology.

4. Fernando La Sama de Araújo
From 26/02/1963 to 02/06/2015.

5. Minister of State, Coordinator of Economic Affairs and Minister of Agriculture and Fisheries
Estanislau da Silva

The Minister of State and Coordinator of Economic Affairs assists the Prime Minister with the supervision of the general policy for the governance of economic affairs, being specifically responsible for the work and activities developed and the provision of related services by the Ministry of Agriculture and Fisheries as the Minister and of Ministry of Agriculture and Fisheries, as the Minister, and the Ministry of Commerce, Industry and Environment, the Ministry of Tourism, Arts and Culture, the Ministry of Public Works, Transports and Communications, the Secretary of State for the Policy of Vocational Training and Employment, the Fishing and cattle farming Industries and the Cooperative Sector.

It is primarily up to the Minister of State and Coordinator of Economic Affairs: to coordinate the preparation and organisation of governmental work for the economic field; to follow-up and assess the works and services provided by the Ministry of Commerce, Industry and Environment; the Ministry of Tourism, Arts and Culture; the Ministry of Public Works, Transports and Communications; the Secretary of State for the Policy of Vocational Training and Employment; the Fishing and cattle farming Industries; and the

Cooperative Sector; to propose and develop public policies in economic areas that account for a better provision of services to the citizens; to propose policies and legislation and lay down mechanisms related with the promotion of private investment, national and international, together with the relevant entities; to promote the development of the national private sector and drawing up policies, support mechanisms and incentives to develop the sector; to promote the dialogue with the national private sector regarding the development of the country and about fighting unemployment; and to uphold the coordination with relevant entities for economic development.

The National Centre for Vocational Training and Employment of Tibar, the National Centre for Vocational Training of Becora, the National Institute for Workforce Development, the Inspectorate-General of Labour, the SERVE Business Registration and Review Service, the Institute of Support to Business Development, the AEI Specialized Investment Agency, the Commercial National Bank of Timor-Leste, PLC, and the Institute of Research, Development, Training and Promotion of Bamboo, Public Institute, are superintended by the Minister of State and Coordinator of Economic Affairs.

As Minister of Agriculture and Fisheries has competences to: propose the policy and draft the regulation projects required for the areas under its responsibility; ensure the implementation and continuity of rural development programs, in coordination with the Ministry of Commerce, Industry and Environment, the Ministry of State Administration and the Government entity responsible for vocational training and employment

Create technical assistance centres for farmers; manage technical and agricultural education; raise agrarian investigation; control the land use for agricultural and livestock purposes; foster and verify animal health; promote the industries of agriculture, livestock and fisheries; foster and oversee food production, including seed production; ensure Quarantine Services; implement a cooperative system for the production and trading of agricultural products; perform feasibility studies for the installation of irrigation systems, water storage and associated facilities.

Manage, in coordination with the Ministry of Commerce, Industry and Environment, forest resources and watersheds; foster the development of industrial plants, namely coffee; Manage water resources for agricultural purposes; control and oversee fisheries and fish farming sectors; lay down coordination and cooperation mechanisms with other Government bodies that supervise related areas; manage National Parks and Protected Areas; and ascertain the protection and preservation of nature and biodiversity, overseeing policy execution and supervising any activities that may hinder the integrity of national fauna and flora, together with related entities.

The Ministry of Agriculture and Fisheries is the central Government body responsible for the design, execution, coordination and assessment of the policy defined and approved by the Council of Ministers for the areas of agriculture, forestry, fisheries and livestock.

6. Minister of State, Coordinator of State Administration Affairs and Justice and Minister of State Administration
Dionísio Babo Soares

The Minister of State and Coordinator of State Administration Affairs and Justice assists the Prime Minister with the supervision of the general policy for the governance of State administration and Justice affairs.

He is responsible for the work and activities developed and for the provision of related services by the Ministry of State Administration, as Minister, and by the Ministry of Justice, the Secretary of State for Institutional Strengthening, the Administrative Decentralisation, the

INAP National Institute for Public Administration, and the State General Inspection.

The Minister of State and Coordinator of State Administration Affairs and Justice has competence to: coordinate the preparation and organisation of governmental work for the State administration and Justice fields; follow-up and assess the works and services provided by the Ministry of Justice; the Secretary of State for Institutional Strengthening; the Administrative Decentralisation; the INAP National Institute for Public Administration; and the State General Inspection; propose and develop public policies for State administration that account for a better provision of services to the citizens.

Support training and permanent assistance to administrative devolution and decentralisation, in coordination with relevant ministries and institutions; promote less bureaucracy and develop the capacity, transparency and efficiency of State administrative services; promote and supervise the entities responsible for training and enhancement of civil servants; develop and implement a scholarship policy that is competitive and transparent; and uphold the coordination with relevant entities for public administration development.

As Minister of State Administration has the following responsibilities: lead the process of administrative decentralization and the setting up of new services and bodies belonging to the Local Government; support permanent training and assistance regarding the devolution and decentralization processes, in coordination with the Ministries and other relevant entities; coordinate and supervise the activities performed by the peripheral services of the Ministry; lay down coordination and cooperation mechanisms with other Public Administration bodies that supervise related areas; propose the public policy and draft the legislation required for the areas under its responsibility.

Suggest and execute the legislation to promote urban hygiene and law and order; propose and implement legal provisions on place names; give technical support to elections and referendums; raise policies of local and rural development, to reduce social and economic inequalities, in cooperation with other governmental bodies for its execution; lay down and implement cooperation and technical support mechanisms to traditional community leaderships; suggest and develop standards and technical instruction to classify, treat and archive historical and State documents; and to promote the recovery, preservation and proper care of historical and State documents.

The Ministry of State Administration supervises the Technical Secretariat for Election Administration, the National Archive and the National Institute of Public Administration.

The Ministry of State Administration is the central Government body responsible for the design, execution, coordination and assessment of the policy defined and approved by the Council of Ministers for the areas of local Government, administrative decentralisation, organisation and execution of elections and referendums, promotion of urban hygiene and organization, and classification and preservation of official documents with historical value.

7. Minister of Foreign Affairs and Cooperation
Hernâni Coelho

The Ministry of Foreign Affairs and Cooperation is the central Government body responsible for the design, execution, coordination and assessment of the policy defined and approved by the Council of Ministers for the areas of international diplomacy and cooperation, consular tasks, and promotion and defence of the Timorese living abroad.

It is incumbent upon the Ministry of Foreign Affairs and Cooperation to: plan, propose and execute the external policy of Timor-Leste, ensuring its unity and consistency; Draft the legal and regulation projects required for the areas under its responsibility; negotiate and recommend the conclusion of international treaties and agreements according to the priorities of external policy for Timor-Leste; promote the external interests of Timor-Leste and protect the Timorese living abroad; represent Timor-Leste in other Countries and International Organizations and manage the network of embassies, missions, permanent and temporary representations and consular posts, according to the priorities of external policy

Plan and prepare the accession of Timor-Leste to the Association of Southeast Asian Nations (ASEAN) and represent the country in several meetings and activities; propose and execute the international cooperation policy, together with the Ministry of Finance and other competent government institutions; coordinate, together with the Ministry of Finance and other competent departments of the Government, the relationship of Timor-Leste with development partners; perform the role committed in terms of economic diplomacy issues; and to lay down coordination and cooperation mechanisms with other Government bodies that supervise related areas.

The Minister of Foreign Affairs and Cooperation supervises the ACTL Cooperation Agency of Timor-Leste.

8. Minister of Finance

Santina Cardoso

The Ministry of Finance is the central Government body responsible for the design, execution, coordination and assessment of the policy defined and approved by the Council of Ministers for the areas of budget and finance annual planning monitoring.

The Minister of Finance has the following responsibilities: propose money and exchange policies in cooperation with the Central Bank; suggest the policy and draft the regulation projects regarding macroeconomics, tax and non-tax revenues, budget framework, public accounting, public finance, auditing and control of the State treasury, issue and management of public debt; manage the petroleum fund of Timor-Leste.

Coordinate the projects and programs between Timor-Leste and development partners, in connection with the Ministry of Foreign Affairs and Cooperation; manage the external public debt, State stake holdings and Development partnerships, through the definition and coordination of tax and financial issues; manage the State assets, without prejudice of the role performed by the Ministry of Justice in terms of real estate; foster the management policy regarding movable assets belonging to the State, in cooperation with other competent public entities; manage the supply of procured goods to all the ministries; negotiate, sign and manage the implementation of contracts for public-private partnerships, ensuring its financial assessment to allow a proper risk-sharing between the State and the private partner and the sustainability of each project; foster the setting up of the National Development Bank; draft and publish official statistics.

Promote the regulation needed and perform the financial control over the State Budget expenses allocated to the other ministries, while pursuing a financial autonomy policy of the services; oversee a correct management of the funding by the State Budget to indirect State administration and local government, through auditing and follow-up; coordinate the national and international technical assistance regarding technical advice to Government bodies, excluding the training of human resources; develop financial management information systems within all services and bodies of the Public Administration, in conjunction with the development of the e-government process; and to lay down coordination and cooperation mechanisms with other Government bodies that supervise related areas.

9. Minister of Justice
Ivo Valente

The Ministry of Justice is the central Government body responsible for the design, execution, coordination and assessment of the policy defined and approved by the Council of Ministers for the areas of justice, land and property, law and human rights.

The Minister of Justice has the following responsibilities: propose the policy and draft the legal and regulation projects required for the areas under its responsibility; suggest measures to define traditional justice mechanisms and its interaction with the formal system; propose and execute measures to broaden the judicial chart; suggest criminal policy and implement it along with good administration of justice; regulate and manage the Legal Training Centre and human resources training for different justice areas

Regulate and manage the penitentiary system, enforcement of penalties and social re-integration services; uphold proper mechanisms of access to the law and the courts, specially to the most underprivileged citizens, regarding legal information and counselling and judicial support, through the Public Defender and other justice entities and structures; set up and assure the proper mechanisms that uphold citizenship rights and promote the release of applicable laws; organise the mapping and registration of land and property, namely real estate.

Ensure a specialized legal translation service to promote official languages in law and justice fields, as a way to foster the access to law by the citizens; manage and supervise registration and notary public services; manage the State real estate; promote and guide the legal training for the judicial careers and remaining civil servants; ascertain international relationships regarding Justice policy, namely with other governments and international organisations, without prejudice of the powers held by the Ministry of Foreign Affairs and Cooperation; and to lay down coordination and cooperation mechanisms with other Government bodies that supervise related areas.

10. Minister of Health
Maria do Céu Sarmento Pina da Costa

The Ministry of Health is the central Government body responsible for design, execution, coordination and assessment of the policy defined and adopted by the Council of Ministers, for the areas of health and pharmaceutical activities.

The Minister of Health is responsible for proposing policy and develop the projects of regulations necessary for the areas under her supervision; ensure access to health care for all citizens; coordinate the activities related to epidemiological control; perform the health control of products with influence on human health; promote the training of health professionals; contribute to the success in humanitarian assistance, promotion of peace, security and socio-economic development, through mechanisms of coordination and collaboration with other Government agencies responsible for related areas.

The Hospitals of the National Health Service and the Autonomous Service of Medicines and Medical Equipment, Public Institute (SAMES), are under the supervision of the Minister of Health.

11. Minister of Social Solidarity
Isabel Amaral Guterres

The Ministry of Social Solidarity is the central Government body responsible for design, execution, coordination and assessment of the policy defined and adopted by the Council of Ministers, for the areas of social security, social assistance, natural disasters and community reinsertion.

The Minister of Social Solidarity has the following responsibilities: design and implement social security systems for workers and rest of the remaining population; develop programs of social assistance and humanitarian aid for the most underprivileged; propose and develop policies and risk management strategies for disasters; develop and implement risk management programs regarding disasters, namely in terms of civic education, prevention, mitigation, urgent response and recovery after disasters; promote programs of demobilization, retirement and pensions for the former National Liberation Fighters; monitor the veterans and National Liberation fighters regarding their integration in society; provide follow-up, protection and community reinsertion of other vulnerable groups; lay down coordination and cooperation mechanisms with other Government bodies that supervise related areas.

The National Centre for Rehabilitation is under the supervision and superintendence of the Minister of Social Solidarity.

12. Minister of Commerce, Industry and Environment
Constâncio da Conceição Pinto

The Ministry of Commerce, Industry and Environment is the central Government body responsible for the design, execution, coordination and assessment of the policy defined and approved by the Council of Ministers for the areas of industrial, and commercial economic activities and co-operative sector, as well as environment.

The Minister of Commerce, Industry and Environment has the following responsibilities: propose the policy and draft the regulation projects required for the areas under his responsibility; design, execute and assess the policies on commerce, industry and environment; add to the growth of economic activity, including national and international competitiveness; support the activities of economic agents, facilitating solutions that render procedural requirements simpler and faster; appraise and license projects of installation and operations for industrial and commercial ventures; inspect and supervise commercial and industrial activities and ventures, in accordance with the law.

Keep and manage an information and documentation centre on companies; propose the qualification and classification of industrial ventures, under the applicable legislation; promote the development of the co-operative sector, specially in rural areas and regarding agriculture, in coordination with the Ministry of Agriculture and Fisheries; promote the importance of the co-operative sector and micro and small enterprises, and promote training on the incorporation, organisation, management and accounting of co-operatives and small companies.

Organize and administer a register of co-operatives; organize and administer the registration of industrial property; promote international and internal rules for standardisation, metrology, and quality control, measurement patterns for units and physical magnitude; implement the environmental policy and assess the results achieved; promote, monitor and support the strategies for the integration of the environment in sectorial policies; Perform the strategic environmental assessment of policies, plans, programs and legislation and coordinate the environmental impact assessments of projects at a national level; Ensure, in general terms and of environmental licensing, the adoption and supervision of pollution prevention and control measures by the relevant facilities.

The National Logistics Centre is under supervision of the Ministry of Commerce, Industry and Environment.

13. António da Conceição
From 16/02/2015 to 10/08/2016day he was sworn in as Minister of State, Coordinator of Social Affairs and Minister of Education.

14. Minister of Tourism, Arts and Culture
Francisco Kalbuady Lay

The Ministry of Tourism, Arts and Culture is the central Government body responsible for the design, execution, coordination and assessment of the policy defined and approved by the Council of Ministers for the areas of tourism, arts and culture.

It is the responsibility of the Minister of Tourism, Arts and Culture to propose policy and develop the projects of regulations necessary for the areas under his supervision; design, execute and evaluate the tourism policy; add to the growth of the tourism sector and suggest measures and public policies for its development; support the activities of economic agents in the tourism sector and facilitate solutions that render licensing procedural requirements simpler and faster; give opinion on requests for information prior to the establishment of tourism businesses; appraise, license projects of facilities and supervise the operation of tourist enterprises; supervise, inspect and monitor recreational games and tourist enterprises, in accordance with the law.

Maintain and administer an information and documentation centre on businesses and activities in the tourism sector; suspend and revoke licenses for the exercise of tourist activities, in accordance with the law; qualify and classify touristic ventures, under the terms of the applicable legislation; draft the annual plan of promotional activities for the development of tourism with respective cost estimate; implement and execute the legislation relating to the installation, licensing, and verification of the conditions of operation of tourist facilities; establish mechanisms for collaboration with other services and government agencies responsible for related areas, in particular the competent services for planning and physical development of the territory, aiming at the promotion of national strategic areas of development of tourism.

Cooperate with concerning public bodies and institutes, in promoting and advertising Timor-Leste with investors and tour operators, releasing the necessary information; oversee cultural and touristic events; draft the policy and regulations for the conservation, protection and preservation of the cultural and historical heritage; propose policies for the definition and development of arts and culture; establish policies of cooperation and cultural exchanges with the CPLP countries and cultural organizations, and countries in the region; establish policies of cooperation with UNESCO.

Promote the creation of the National Library and the National Museum; develop programs to introduce artistic education and culture in the education curricula of Timor-Leste, in coordination with the Ministry of Education; promote the creative industries and artistic creation in Timor-Leste, in its several areas; ensure the adequate preservation of official and historical documents; promote the creation of the Academy of Arts and Cultural Creative Industries of Timor-Leste; protect the rights pertaining to artistic and literary creation.

The Convention Centre of Dili-CCD, the Catering Squares/Food Courts (Metiaut), the Centres of Tourism and Tourist Information, the Implementation Unit of the Academy of Arts, Culture and Creative

Industries and the Monitoring Committee of the Academy of Arts, Culture and Creative Industries are supervised by the Minister of Tourism, Arts and Culture.

15. Minister of Public Works, Transport and Communications
Gastão de Sousa

The Ministry of Public Works, Transport and Communications is the central Government body responsible for the design, execution, coordination and assessment of the policy defined and approved by the Council of Ministers for the areas of public works, housing, supply, distribution and management of water, sanitation and electricity, transport and communications.

It is incumbent upon the Minister of Public Works, Transport and Communications to propose and execute the policy lines of the Ministry in the areas of public works, housing, water supply, water resource management, sanitation and electricity; propose and execute the policy lines of the Ministry in the areas of transport and communications; ensure the implementation and enforcement of the legal and regulatory framework related to the activities of the ministry; create and implement the legal and regulatory framework of the activity of the construction industry and research on construction materials.

Study and perform the works of protection, conservation and repair of bridges, roads, river and sea coasts, in particular concerning flood control; promote the study and implementation of the new Systems of infrastructure networks for distribution of water and water resources, as well as sanitation, and monitor their operation and exploration, without prejudice to the powers committed in these areas to other bodies; establish coordination and promote the quality of physical projects executed by the State.

Promote the implementation of works of construction, maintenance and repair of public buildings, monuments and special installations, in the cases in which it is the Ministry's legal responsibility; license and inspect all urban construction, including by private, municipal or autonomous entities, in the terms of the applicable legislation; promote the adoption of technical standards and regulations relating to materials used in the construction industry, as well as develop laboratory tests to guarantee the safety of building.

Maintain and develop a national system of monitoring and information on the state of construction works and on the materials used in construction, including the effects of floods in infrastructures; ensure the coordination of the renewable energy sector and stimulate complementarity between its various modes, as well as their competitiveness, in order to better satisfy users; regulate, in coordination with other ministries, operators in the area of electricity production; establish mechanisms for collaboration and coordination with other Government bodies responsible for related areas; develop and regulate communications activities, and optimize the means of communication.

Ensure the coordination of the transport sector and stimulate the complementarity between its various modes, as well as their competitiveness, in order to better satisfy users; promote management, as well as the adoption of technical standards and regulations regarding the use of public communications services; ensure the provision of public telecommunications services, and the use of radio-electric space through public enterprises or by granting the provision of public service to private entities; maintain and develop the national systems of weather and seismological information and monitoring, including the construction and maintenance of its infrastructure, and promote and coordinate scientific research and technological development in the fields of civilian land, air and maritime transport.

The Minister for Public Works, Transport and Communications has authority over the Administration of Ports of Timor-Leste - APORTIL,

Administration of Airports and Air Navigation - ANATL E. P., the Civil Aviation Authority of Timor-Leste - AACTL, ARC-Regulatory Authority for Telecommunications and the Institute for Equipment Management - IGE.

16. Minister of Petroleum and Mineral Resources
Alfredo Pires

The Ministry of Petroleum and Mineral Resources is the central Government body responsible for the design and execution of the energy policy and management of mineral resources, including oil and other strategic minerals, as approved by the Council of Ministers, as well as for licensing and regulation of extractive activities, industrial activities of improvement of oil and minerals, including the petrochemical and refining industry.

The Minister of Petroleum and Mineral Resources is responsible for: draft and propose the policy and legislation for the sector; establish the sectorial management system and regulate its activities; ensure maximum participation of Timor-Leste in oil and mineral resources activities through the proper legal, administrative and technical instruments; promote national opportunities in this sector in order to capture and consolidate related foreign investment; monitor treaty implementation and follow the execution of relevant sectorial instruments; In coordination with relevant ministries and entities, conduct negotiations regarding the development model of the "Greater Sunrise" field or other issues related with the jurisdiction over the Timor Sea; coordinate the execution of the '

Tasi Mane' project and license and monitor the activities developed in territorial areas dedicated to the project; determine, in accordance with the general conditions determined by law, the contractual terms specific to prospecting and exploration of petroleum resources and mining licensing; ensure minimum reserves of fuel and its regular supply to public entities in charge of energy production; regulate, authorize and supervise "downstream" activities, namely export, transport, storage, distribution and trading, wholesale and retail, including the import of crude oil, derived products and minerals.

Authorize and license manufacturing industry projects located downstream to extraction regarding the processing, upgrading, treatment and conversion of crude oil, oil products and minerals, namely refineries, liquefaction plants, gas or petrochemical; taking into account the complexity and technical expertise associated with the oil and mineral resources sector, approve the environmental licenses in coordination with the competent authorities in the area of Environment; exercise the supervision and superintendence powers over the indirect administration, institutions and State enterprises and develop the knowledge and research of the geological structure of the soil and subsoil and the national hydrogeological resources.

The following entities are under the supervision of the Minister of Oil and Mineral Resources: National Authority of Oil and Minerals, Timor Gap, E. P., the Institute of Petroleum and Geology, I. P. and the Mines of Timor, S.A..

17. Minister of Defence
Cirilo Cristóvão

The Ministry of Defence is the central Government body responsible for the design, execution, coordination and evaluation of policy, defined and adopted by the Council of Ministers, for the areas of national defence and military cooperation.

It is incumbent upon the Minister of Defence to propose and execute the policy relating to the military component of national defence; draft the regulations necessary to the Defence area; promote military strategic diplomacy, coordinating and guiding the activities arising from military commitments under instruments of international law and multilateral/bilateral agreements, as well as the military relationships with States and international organizations, without prejudice of the powers conferred to the Ministry of Foreign Affairs and Cooperation.

Ensure defence-related relationships with other countries and international organizations, without prejudice of the powers conferred to the Ministry of Foreign Affairs and Cooperation, under the aims set by the Timorese foreign policy; coordinate and monitor, together with the Ministry of Foreign Affairs and Cooperation, cooperation actions developed by international organizations, States and Defence forces and services of other countries to support the development of the areas under its responsibility, under the international agreements indicated above; administer and supervise the Defence Forces of Timor-Leste; promote the adequacy of military resources and monitor and inspect its use; exercise supervision, administer and monitor the Maritime Authority; supervise military related sea and air navigation and establish mechanisms for cooperation and coordination with other Government bodies responsible for related areas.

The Minister of Defence also supervises the Institute for National Defence.

18. Minister of the Interior
Longuinhos Monteiro

The Ministry of the Interior is the central Government body responsible for the design, execution, coordination and evaluation of policy, defined and adopted by the Council of Ministers, for the areas of internal security, of migration and border control, the civil protection and police cooperation.

It is incumbent upon the Minister of the Interior to propose, coordinate and implement the policies on internal security and civil protection; participate in the definition, coordination and execution of national security policy; draft the regulations needed for the areas under its responsibility; supervise and manage the forces and services of security of Timor-Leste; supervise and manage the Civil Protection Authority, including the Fire Department; ensure and keep public law and order.

Uphold the freedom and safety of people and their assets; ensure the safety of movable and immovable State assets; prevent and repress criminality; control the movement of people across borders, the entry, presence, residence, departure and expulsion of foreign people from the national territory; control the import, production, trading, licensing, possession and use of weapons, ammunition and explosives, without prejudice of the powers conferred to other Government bodies; regulate, supervise and control private security activities;

supervise civilian sea and air navigation; prevent disasters and serious accidents and provide protection and assistance to populations affected in the event of fires, floods, landslides, earthquakes and in all the situations that put them at risk

Develop, in coordination with other competent entities, civic education programs to face natural disasters or man-made disasters, cementing social solidarity; coordinate and monitor the Municipal Security Councils; promote the development of the strategy for prevention, mediation and resolution of community conflicts; promote adequate police means and inspect their use; ensure internal security related relationships with other countries and international organizations, without prejudice of the powers conferred to the Ministry of Foreign Affairs and Cooperation, under the goals set by the Timorese foreign policy.

Negotiate, under the leadership of the President of the Republic and the Prime-Minister and in coordination with the Ministry of Foreign Affairs and Cooperation, international agreements about matters under its responsibility, namely regarding internal security, criminal investigation, migration, border control and civil protection; coordinate and monitor, in coordination with the Ministry of Foreign Affairs and Cooperation, cooperation actions developed by international organizations, States, or security forces and services of other countries, in support to the development of its areas of responsibility, in the context of international agreements indicated above, and establish mechanisms for cooperation and coordination with other Government bodies responsible for related areas.

19. Minister of Planning and Strategic Investment
Kay Rala Xanana Gusmão

The Ministry of Planning and Investment Strategy is the central Government body responsible for the design, execution, coordination and evaluation of policy, defined and adopted by the Council of Ministers, for the areas of promotion of economic and social development of the country.

Through strategic and integrated planning and the rationalization of available financial resources, the Minister of Planning and Strategic Investment takes on specific responsibilities over the implementation of the Strategic Development Plan, particularly in relation to Infrastructure and Urban Planning, Petroleum and Mineral Resources, and Territorial Planning.

It is incumbent upon the Minister of Planning and Strategic Investment, the responsibility over the quality of work and activities for the implementation of physical projects of the Special Funds and other construction works, National Procurement Commission NPC, and National Development Agency - NDA.

On the basis of the statistical data and records made available by the competent services, it is incumbent upon the Minister of Planning and Strategic Investment to assess the development capital projects, based on careful analysis of the feasibility of the projects and on their respective cost-benefit; supervise, monitor and certify the implementation and execution of the projects, thus contributing to the rationalize the available financial resources, and to the economic development and the economic activity at national, provincial and local level; plan and control costs and quality of development capital projects; promote transparency and quality through the provision of procurement services for development capital projects; develop studies, opinions and technical and sectorial analyses in order to assess the impact and economic viability of development projects; review and select proposals for investment in the country.

Ensure the coordination and the implementation of Planning for District Integrated Development, in coordination with the relevant entities; ensure the coordination and implementation of the National Program for Suco Development; develop and implement policies and mechanisms to support community and suco development; develop the Program Millennium Development Goals Sucos (MDG Sucos); study, plan and propose policies for sectorial development; study, plan, and propose a national housing and spatial planning policy; study, plan and propose the urban planning, throughout the territory; propose and develop a national policy for natural resources and minerals.

Support and develop the legal framework and regulate activities related to renewable energy resources; support studies on the capacity of renewable energy resources and alternative energy sources; maintain a record of information about renewable energy operations and resources; contribute to the development of the national policy on transport and communications; help prepare and develop, in cooperation with other public services, the implementation of the road plan for the national territory; provide support for the coordination and promotion of a management system, maintenance and modernization of the airport infrastructure, air navigation, roads, port and related services, and propose and develop a policy of training of human resources, taking into account the needs in the short, medium and long term, and in areas that are crucial to the Development of the country.

The Minister of Planning and Strategic Investment supervises the National Procurement Commission - CNA, the National Development Agency NDA, the Secretariat of Major Projects and the Mission Unit for Integrated Regional Development - TIA.

20. Vice Minister of Education I
Dulce Jesus Soares

21. Vice Minister of Education II
Abel da Costa Ximenes

22. Vice Minister of Agriculture and Fisheries
Marcos da Cruz

23. Vice Minister of State Administration
Tomás do Rosário Cabral

24. Vice Minister of Foreign Affairs and Cooperation
Roberto Sarmento de Oliveira Soares

The Vice Minister for Foreign Affairs and Cooperation supports the Minister of Foreign Affairs and Cooperation, overseeing the Administration, Planning and Finance, Human Resources and Legal Affairs Services integrated in direct administration of his Ministry.

The Vice Minister for Foreign Affairs and Cooperation is also responsible for services that deal with the consular affairs and protocol, and by all the diplomatic and cooperation matters relating to the Association of Southeast Asian Nations (ASEAN).

25. Vice Minister of Finance
Hélder Lopes

The Vice Minister of Finance supports the Minister of Finance in the management of the external affairs of the Ministry, including relations with international organizations and national entities, as well as the coordination of the projects and programs between Timor-Leste and the development partners, in liaison with the Ministry of Foreign Affairs and Cooperation.

The Vice Minister of Finance oversees the preparation and publication of official statistics, as well as other documents prepared by the Ministry of Finance, notably the books of the General State Budget, information for planning and budget implementation reports, among others.

It is his responsibility to coordinate the communication and public relations of the Ministry of Finance and manage political affairs, as well as the connection of the Ministry with the National Parliament and the respective special committees, in terms of the legislative proposals and the provision of information in the Finance portfolio.

The Vice Minister of Finance also oversees the implementation of the tax reform approved by the Council of Ministers.

26. Vice Minister of Health

Ana Isabel Soares

27. Vice Minister of Social Solidarity
Miguel Marques Manetelu

28. Vice Minister of Commerce, Industry and the Environment
Filipus Nino Pereira

29. Constâncio da Conceição Pinto
From 16/02/2015 to 10/08/2016 day he was sworn in as Minister of Commerce, Industry and Environment.

30. Vice Minister of Public Works, Transport and Communications I
Januário da Costa Pereira

The Vice Minister of Public Works, Transport and Communications I supports the Minister of Public Works, Transport and Communications in the supervision of the internal services responsible for the areas of electricity, water and sanitation.

31. Vice Minister of Public Works, Transport and Communication II
Inácio Moreira

The Vice Minister of Public Works, Transport and Communications II supports the Minister of Public Works, Transport and Communications in the supervision of the internal services responsible for the areas of the land, maritime and air transport, meteorology and geophysics, and postal services.

The Vice Minister of Public Works, Transport and Communications II has, by delegation, the responsibility of the Port Administration in Timor-Leste (PATL), the Public Company of Airports Administration and Air Navigation of Timor-Leste, the Civil Aviation Authority of Timor-Leste and of the National Communications Authority (NCA).

32. Secretary of State for the Council of Ministers
Avelino Maria Coelho da Silva

The Secretary of State for the Council of Ministers supports the Prime Minister and the Minister of State and of the Presidency of the Council of Ministers, regarding the coordination of the legislative procedure of the Government.

Specifically, he is responsible: to coordinate the drafting and analysis of legal and regulatory projects of the Government, promoting quality, harmonization and simplification of legal and regulatory acts; to coordinate the approval procedure and publication of legal diplomas, ensuring the procedural requirements in hearings for both public and private bodies; translate or follow the translation of legal drafts or other documents needed by the Presidency of the Council of Ministers (PCM) and by the Prime Minister; ensure the provision of legal, informative, technical and administrative support to the Council of Ministers, to the Prime Minister, to the Minister of State and remaining members of the Government integrated within the PCM and assess the impact of legislative acts.

The supervision over the National Printing is delegated to the Secretary of State for the Council of Ministers.

33. Secretary of State for Parliamentary Affairs
Maria Terezinha Viegas

The Secretary of State for Parliamentary Affairs assists the Prime Minister in the Government's relations with the National Parliament and with the parliamentary benches.

Specifically, it is the responsibility of the Secretary of State for Parliamentary Affairs: to represent the Government in meetings with the Conference of Representatives of the Parliamentary Benches and other parliamentary bodies, including the Bureau; when requested, represent the Government by issuing legal opinions on legislative, resolution and parliamentary monitoring procedures, where the Government should participate or be called upon.

Regularly accompany the referred procedures, gathering all the information it deems necessary to keep the Government informed of the development of the various procedural stages; draft information, prepare documentation and draft instrumental notes concerning every relevant activity under the National Parliament, which is not of a purely internal character, to scheduling legislative and resolution initiatives and coordination between the two organs of sovereignty; represent the Government and collaborate, when expressly requested, in the final drafting of legislative acts or resolutions of the National Parliament, that require publication in the Jornal da República (Official Gazette) and keep a documentation and information archive on parliamentary affairs, in order to be able to inform the Government, at any time, on any affair related to the National Parliament.

The supervision of the Office to the Parliamentary Affairs is delegated to the Secretary of State for Parliamentary Affairs.

34. Secretary of State for Social Communication
Nélio Isaac Sarmento

The Secretary of State for Media assists the Prime Minister and the Minister of the Presidency of the Council of Ministers in the Media sector having competencies to promote the development and regulation of the engagement of the media, particularly the press, radio and television.

Specifically, it is the responsibility of the Secretary of State for Media: to coordinate the dissemination of information on Government programs and actions, ensuring transparency and access to information; design, execute and assess public policies for the media; promote and develop the news agency of Timor-Leste and exercise supervision over the State media bodies.

The supervision of both the National Directorate of Dissemination and Information and the Community Radio Centre is delegated to the Secretary of State for Media as well as the superintendence of RTTL - Rádio e Televisão de Timor-Leste, EP.

35. Secretary of State for the Support and Socio-Economical Promotion of Women
Veneranda Lemos Martins

36. Secretary of State Youth and Sports
Leovigildo Hornay

37. Secretary of State for Employment Policy and Vocational Training
Ilídio Ximenes da Costa

39. Secretary of State for State Administration
Samuel Mendonça

40. Secretary of State for Land and Property
Jaime Xavier Lopes

41. Secretary of State for Arts and Culture
Maria Isabel de Jesus Ximenes

Economy

Prior to and during colonisation Timor was best known for its sandalwood. In late 1999, about 70% of the economic infrastructure of East Timor was laid waste by Indonesian troops and anti-independence militias, and 260,000 people fled westward. Over the next three years a massive international program led by the UN, manned by civilian advisers, 5,000 peacekeepers (8,000 at peak) and 1,300 police officers, led to substantial reconstruction in both urban and rural areas. By mid-2002, all but about 50,000 of the refugees had returned. This successful UN effort was headed by Special Representative of the Secretary-General, Sérgio Vieira de Mello, later to become High Commissioner for Human Rights, who was killed in Baghdad in August 2003.

The country faces great challenges in continuing the rebuilding of infrastructure and the strengthening of the infant civil administration. One promising long-term project is the joint development with

Australia of petroleum and natural gas resources in the south-eastern waters off Timor, a location which became known as the Timor gap following the signing by Australia and Indonesia of the 'Timor Gap Treaty' when East Timor was still under Indonesian occupation.

East Timor inherited no permanent maritime boundaries when it attained independence, and the Government of East Timor is seeking to negotiate a boundary with Australia halfway between it and Australia. As at May 2004, the Government of Australia wanted to establish the boundary at the end of the Australian continental shelf. Normally a maritime dispute such as this could be referred to the International Court of Justice or the International Tribunal for the Law of the Sea for an impartial decision. However Australia withdrew from these organisations when it realised that East Timor might invoke these dispute resolution mechanisms.

Many advocacy groups claimed that Australia deliberately obstructed negotiations because the existing arrangement benefited Australia financially. On July 7, 2005, an agreement was finally reached under which both countries would set aside the dispute over the maritime boundary, and East Timor would receive A$13 billion (US$9.65 billion) in revenue.

Currently three foreign banks have a branch in Dili: ANZ Bank, Banco Nacional Ultramarino, and Bank Mandiri.

East Timor has the lowest per capita income in the world (USD 400 per annum) according to the CIA World Factbook, 2005.

Australia and East Timor officials signed a billion-dollar gas and oil accord, which is necessary because of a current maritime border dispute between the countries, which covers a major oil field. Although the accord has to be ratified by East Timor's parliament which is ruled by Fretilin with 55 seats the biggest block in parliament, but all the smaller parties are said to be working together to veto the deal.

In 1975, Portugal abandoned East Timor and the people declared self-independence only to be invaded by Indonesia with out any intervention from Australia or the United States. Indonesia then agreed on no formal maritime boards but on a joint exploitation zone splitting profits 50/50. Indonesian rule in East Timor was marked by extreme violence and brutality and following a UN-sponsored agreement between Indonesia, Portugal and the US, East Timor held a referendum and gained independence, but violent Indonesian sponsored militia took hold. A peacekeeping force (INTERFET, led by Australia) then intervened putting a stop to the violence. The exploitation zone splitting profits was then changed to 60% in favour of Australia, but now a new deal has been proposed 90/10 in favour of Timor. In the mean time Australia has been accused of profiting by up to 2 billion dollars between the deals by activist groups like http://www.timorseajustice.org/ whose campaigning saw Woodside suspended oil pumping in the affected area.

Contemporary International law asserts that the area under dispute belongs to East Timor. Australia has withdrawn from the maritime division of the International Court of Justice, which could have settled this matter, instead opting to try to settle the matter without the court.

The previous deal has caused political infighting within East Timor about why such a smaller percentage was accepted.

Telecommunications

Following Indonesian withdrawal from East Timor in 1999, the telecommunications infrastructure was destroyed in the ensuing violence. A new country calling code (670) was allocated to East Timor, but international access often remains severely limited. A complicating factor is the fact that 670 was previously used by the Northern Marianas, with many carriers not aware that the code is now used by

East Timor. (The Northern Marianas, now part of the North American Numbering Plan, use the code 1 and the area code 670.)

It is also often extremely expensive: for example, Telstra in Australia raised the cost of calls to East Timor to A$3.00 a minute from 97 cents in 2003. In the UK, BT's standard rate is £2 a minute.

Telstra expanded its cellular telephone signal into East Timor in 2000, and operated services until 2003, when Timor Telecom, 50.1% part-owned by Portugal Telecom, began operating fixed line and mobile telephone services. Until recently, the fixed line network was mainly confined to the capital Dili, although this has been expanded nationwide, to each district capital.

According to a press-release issued by Portugal Telecom, the total number of fixed phones (landline) are 2,100, mobile cellular are 25,000, 500 Dial-up access users and 30 broadband users (as of October 2004).

Portugal Telecom signed a 15-year contract in 2002 to invest US$ 29 million to rebuild and operate the phone system. The contract could be extended by 10 more years, totalling 25 years of monopoly. 2003 gross revenue totalled € 10.5 million.

All voice and data are carried out by Intelsat, using a direct satellite link with one hop to their downlink in Portugal.

Telephones - main lines in use:

2,100 (as per Timor Telecom press-release from Oct 2004)

Telephones - mobile cellular:

25,000 (as per Timor Telecom press-release from Oct 2004)

Radio broadcast stations:

AM NA, FM NA, shortwave NA

The main station is Radio Timor Leste, broadcasting in Tetum, Portuguese and Indonesian. Other radio stations include Radio Kmanek, and Radio Falintil, and Radio Renascença, while there are also FM retransmissions of RDP Internacional from Portugal and Radio Australia.

Television broadcast stations:

1 Televisão Timor Leste or Televizaun Timor Lorosae - broadcasts local programming, as well as retransmissions of RTP Portugal, ABC Asia Pacific from Australia and BBC World from the UK. The TV signal is confined to Dili.

Internet country code:

.TP is the Internet top-level domain code used for East Timor, based on its previous ISO 3166-1 code. However, the latter code was officially changed to TL when the country achieved its independence on May 20, 2002, and during the course of 2005, internet domains will change from '.tp' to '.tl'.

Internet Service Providers (ISPs):

Timor Telecom is an ISP itself along with one downstream provider, iNet. The latter only offers services in the capital, Dili. 2-way Satellite Internet is in theory available as the country falls within the Australia and Asia footprints of several satellites offering this service, however in practice licenses are not granted for use of non-Timor Telecom services. As such, internet services are restricted to locations with landline telephone or DSL infrastructure. WiMAX and GPRS internet access are not available.

Voice over IP

Timor Telecom has sought to block some Voice over IP services on its network such as Skype, and as a result some such services may not function.

Internet users:

Dial-up: 2,100 (as per Timor Telecom press-release from Oct 2004)
Broadband: 50 (as per Timor Telecom press-release from Oct 2004)

Oil

Timor Leste, as one the poorest nations in the Southeast Asian region, has pinned much of its hopes for economic development and self-reliance on the off-shore gas and oil reserves in the Timor Sea. East Timor's oil resources have historically attracted international interest, especially from Indonesia and Australia. On-going current negotiations and disagreements, however, continue between Timor Leste and Australia. This section provides a brief overview of the oil issue, which was also an aspect of the major powers' acquiescence to Indonesian invasion of East Timor in 1975.

In December 1974 Portugal was already negotiating agreements on off-shore oil concessions in the Timor Sea with American oil companies Adobe Gas and Oceanic Company of Denver (Taylor 1994:37). These agreements were later reversed as a consequence of political lobbying by Australia. A year earlier, Australia and Indonesia had a tentative agreement on the maritime boundary in the Timor Sea already which could not be finalized as parts of it came under Portuguese Timor's jurisdiction (ibid:38).

Thus, in 1975 Australia seemed to support the integration of East Timor with Indonesia, in order to endure their access to maritime oil and wanted to rapidly secure the maritime boundary with Indonesia (ibid:75). BHP oil company was a strong Australian Oil interest lobbyer in this matter. In 1988, the Australian government has come to an agreement of cooperation with the Indonesian military on the exploitation of Timor Gap oil resources (ibid:164). Australian economic interests tended to influence their policy towards East Timor during the 1980s. On 11 December 1989 Timor Gap Treaty came into existence in which Indonesia and Australia divided the area into oil exploration zones.

This agreement continues to be renegotiated between Australia and East Timor as a consequence of the country's separation from Indonesia. Hill and Saldanha (2001:18) highlight some of the difficulties concerning the Timor Gap negotiations during the time of the UN transitional administration. For one thing the reserves were yet to be fully prospected. The maritime border between the two countries was yet to be settled.

The royalty split was projected to be 85:15 percent in East Timor's favour. This precipitated a rather optimistic projection for the annual economic growth rate of 15 percent for nine years by the World Bank mission in East Timor (Soesantro 2001:88). In 2001 many East Timorese felt that the 85:15 split was highly unfair and rather exploitative in nature for the new nation. During July 2001, prior to the Constituent Assembly elections, this issue was raised numerous times during public consultation and voter education meetings even in remote villages. The East Timorese people were keenly aware of the possible economic resources for their new nation, particularly oil. Even illiterate villagers were aware of the proposed 85:15 split and expressed their disappointment. Indeed, during my long-term election observation period I witnessed in one village in the Aileu district a 'town hall meeting' during a brief visit of a high ranking UN official. The main issue the villagers wanted the official to address was the oil resource issue and how East Timor can become self-sufficient in the future with such unfair and exploitative proposition

Australia was not prepared for the robust negotiations by East Timor Formal negotiations began in October 2000 and Australia signed the New Timor Sea Treaty with a 90:10 split in East Timor's favour on 20 May 2002. One sticky point however remained and that concerned the maritime boundaries. Australia strongly opposed the formerly negotiated boundaries with Indonesia. East Timor on the other hand bid for a boundary that was half-way between the two countries. East Timor wished that the International Court of Justice arbitrate the boundary dispute, however, Australia dismissed this and withdrew from ICJ section that deals with maritime boundary disputes two months prior to East Timorese independence. The boundary that East

Timor desires would also aid in tripling its oil revenue. Article 22 of the Timor Sea Treaty that was signed in 2002 provides for a 30 year duration unless the boundary settled sooner between the two countries. Since the treaty was signed East Timor has argued that,

Under current principles of international law, it is entitled to a greater share of the Timor Sea's oil and gas resources than is suggested by the boundaries of the Timor Sea Treaty's Joint Petroleum Development Area ("JPDA"). Principally, East Timor Asserts that the western and eastern lines defining the JPDA are ill-founded at international law, a claim that has immediate implications for the joint venture partners in the Greater Sunrise fields that straddle the JPDA's eastern boundary.

The boundary dispute is likely to be a complicated and drawn-out affair between the two countries. Earlier this year (2005), East Timor's parliament refused to pass legislation to support the Greater Sunrise project until the dispute was resolved. The project was then put on hold by the global oil and gas companies (Woodside, Conoco Phillips, Shell and Osaka Gas). The Timor Sea Justice Coalition also spearheaded a community campaign for a just settlement from the Australian government. This coalition also estimates that if the boundary were half-way between the two countries, East Timor would gain substantial gas and oil royalties (about $40 billion)

Most recent negotiations have not settled the maritime boundary issue. However, it has been reported that Australia changed its original offer to East Timor from 18% to a 50% share of the royalties from the proposed development of Woodside Petroleum Group's Greater Sunrise gas-condensate field. The final details of the negotiations and prospective deal are not yet available at the time of writing. However, on 17 May 2005 some news sources suggested that for a further $3.8 billion royalty revenue all East Timor would have to do is to defer any final maritime boundary settlement for fifty years. East Timor as the cash-strapped and poorest nation of Southeast Asia might be thus forced into an inequitable settlement, depending on the negotiating tenacity of its leadership

People and Culture

The culture of East Timor reflects numerous cultural influences, including Portuguese, Roman Catholic and Malay, on the indigenous Austronesian cultures of Timor. Legend tells that a giant crocodile was transformed into the island of Timor, or Crocodile Island, as it is often called. Like Indonesia, the culture of East Timor has been heavily influenced by Austronesian legends, although the Catholic influence is stronger, the population being mainly Roman Catholic.

Illiteracy is still widespread, but there is a strong tradition of poetry. As for architecture, some Portuguese-style buildings can be found, although the traditional totem houses of the eastern region, known as uma lulik also survive. Craftmanship is also widespread, as is the weaving of traditional scarves or tais.

Literature

Easily the most famous East Timorese author is Xanana Gusmão, the leader of the Timorese resistance organization Fretilin, and now the president of independent East Timor. He wrote two books during the struggle for independence. Also a poet and painter, he produced works describing the culture, values, and skills of the Timorese people.

Other important writers of Timor are: Fernando Sylvan, Francisco Borja da Costa, Ruy Cinatti, and Fitun Fuik.

Music

East Timor's music reflects its history under the control of both Portugal and Indonesia, who have imported music like gamelan and fado. The most widespread form of native folk music was the likurai dance, performed to by women to welcome home men after war. They used a small drum and sometimes carried enemy heads in processions through villages; a modern version of the dance is used by women in courtship.

In the modern era, Timorese music has been closely associated with the independence movement; for example, the band Dili All Stars released a song that became an anthem in the build-up to the referendum on independence in 2000, while the United Nations commissioned a song called "Hakotu Ba" (by Lahane) to encourage people to register to vote in the referendum.

East Timorese popular musicians include Teo Batiste Ximenes, who grew up in Australia and uses folk rhythms from his homeland in his music. With many East Timorese people in emigrant communities in Australia, Portugal and elsewhere, East Timorese folk music has been brought to many places around the world. Refugee camps in Portugal mixed together East Timorese music with styles from other Portuguese colonies like Angola and Mozambique.

The guitar has long been an important part of East Timorese musc, though it is an import brought by colonizers; there, however, native kinds of string instruments similar in some ways to the guitar. Foreign influences also include popular styles of music like rock and roll, hip hop and reggae.

Religion

East Timor has been nominally Catholic since early in the Portuguese colonial period. The Catholic faith became a central part of East Timorese culture during the Indonesian occupation between 1975 and 1999. While under Portuguese rule, the East Timorese had mostly been animist, sometimes integrated with minimal Catholic ritual, the number of Catholics dramatically increased under Indonesian rule. This was for several reasons: Indonesia was predominantly Muslim; the Indonesian state required adherence to one of five officially recognised religions and did not recognise traditional beliefs; and because the Catholic church, which remained directly responsible to the Vatican throughout Indonesian rule, became a refuge for East Timorese seeking sanctuary from persecution.

The 'Apostolic Administrator' (de facto Bishop) of the Diocese of Dili, Monsignor Martinho da Costa Lopes, began speaking out against human rights abuses by the Indonesian security forces, including rape, torture, murder, and disappearances. Following pressure from Jakarta, he stepped down in 1983 and was replaced by the younger priest, Monsignor Carlos Felipe Ximenes Belo, who Indonesia thought would be more loyal. However, he too began speaking out, not only against human rights abuses, but the issue of self-determination, writing an open letter to the Secretary General of the United Nations, calling for a referendum. In 1996 he was awarded the Nobel Peace Prize, along with exiled leader José Ramos Horta, now the country's Foreign Minister.

In spite of accusations by the Suharto regime that East Timor's independence movement, Fretilin, was communist, many of its leaders had trained to be priests, and their philosophy probably owed more to the Catholic liberation theology of Latin America than to Marxism.

However, in spite of the majority of the country's people now being Catholics, there is freedom of religion in the new republic, and the Prime Minister Marí Alkatiri, is a Muslim of Yemeni descent.

Religion in more Detail
Catholicism and Ancestral Cults
The majority of the population is Roman Catholic. According to the 2002 diocese statistics, 749,000 of the country's total population of 792,000 are Roman Catholics. Current statistics are not yet available about the other religious minorities represented in East Timor, mainly Protestants, Muslims and Hindu-Buddhists. Small concentrations of Protestants (around 20,000) have been reported in Maliana, Aileu, and Baucau as well as in Dili. A smattering of Muslims and Buddhists are also present in Dili.

Current numbers are difficult to estimate for these other religions, since most of their adherents were primarily ethnically non-East Timorese who departed after the 1999 separation from Indonesia. During the past three decades, the Catholic religion played an important part in the lives of East Timorese. The Constitution of this new nation, which was ratified on 22 March 2002, under Section 12 recognizes religious freedom and tolerance as long as religious activities are in "due observance of the Constitution and the law." Furthermore, paragraph 2 of Section 12 declares, "The State shall promote the cooperation with the different religious denominations that contribute to the well-being of the people of East Timor".

In the literature, there has been virtually nothing reported about the practices of Protestant, Muslim, and Hindu-Buddhist minorities in terms of the uniquely East Timorese features of these religions. Protestant missionary groups operate in small numbers in East Timor, however, exact figures are unavailable and it is estimated that after independence the size of the congregation was halved. In 2000 there were about 20,000 church members and only seven pastors to serve them. With the exception of minor tensions in Baucau region between Protestant missionaries and Catholics, the two Christian branches appear to coexist peacefully.

Minor isolated incidences of violence have been reported against Muslim mosques in the capital city Dili and in Baucau. There have also been tensions reported between Muslims of Arabic descent and Muslims of Malay migrant descent. Unlike other World Religions, animism, mainly focusing on ancestral beliefs has been documented in

Portuguese colonial writings. Even currently practiced Catholicism is a highly syncretized or indigenized religion—indigenized through the lenses of traditional cosmologies and belief systems of the East Timorese.

Catholicism, introduced by the Portuguese during the 16th century, initially spread to the more accessibly coastal regions while the mountainous interior provided a geographical barrier (Felgas 1956; Matos 1974; Vasconcelos 1937). After the 1975 Indonesian invasion, 72% of the population still remained animist. While the Portuguese brought Catholicism to East Timor by the 16th century, by the 1975 invasion of Indonesia, the majority (72%) of the population remained animist.

This period precipitated a steady stream of conversion to Catholicism among the East Timorese. The importance of Catholicism grew during the Indonesian occupation throughout East Timor in terms of a huge conversion success. The Church was the main provider of protection, the vehicle of non-violent protest and critique of brutalities, as well as the rallying point for the freedom fighting movement (see for example, Carrey 1999; Gunn 2001; Kohen 1998, 2001; Lenox 2000).

Roman Catholicism was introduced to East Timor by the Portuguese by 1515. However, the 1556 arrival of the Dominican friar, António

Taveira, marked officially the commencement of a more widespread missionising effort. The East Timorese were never forced to convert however if a local chief converted many of his people would convert as well, therefore the Church's effort concentrated on the north and south coastal kingdoms during the late 16th century. By 1640 there were 10 missions and 22 churches on Timor. The next wave of expansion of the faith began in 1697 with the return of Friar Manuel de Santo António to Timor. By 1702 the Carmelite order was also present in East Timor.

By 1747 there were two seminaries established in Timor, in Oecussi and in Manatuto. The missionising work of the Dominican friars, however, was hampered by a rather tense relationship with the colonial administrative government on East Timor. In 1834 the Dominicans were expelled from East Timor and were replaced by the Jesuit order. The Jesuits' activities were not successful until the latter part of the 19th century. In addition to Church-State relations, missionising was also curtailed by the long history of East Timorese rebellions against colonial exploitation.

From the earliest times, however, the Church has been an important supporter of the native populations against such exploitations. Rebellions against the colonial power structure were often linked to a great variety of revitalization movements throughout history. The Canossian order of nuns returned to Timor in the early 1920s and the Salesian and Jesuit orders returned after the Japanese occupation of WW II. After the Second Vatican council the Portuguese language was replaced by the Tetum language (1981) as the Catholic rites became vernacularized.

While this contributed to the Church's headways in conversion rates, substantial success did not occur until after the post-colonial Indonesian invasion in 1975 when the Catholic Church ceased to a part of the Portuguese Catholic Church. The Catholic Church became the protector of the masses providing physical refuge and moral support against the brutality of the occupation, and thus incidentally becoming the rallying point for resistance.

The major waves of concentrated efforts in spreading Catholicism in East Timor can be attributed to Friar António Taveira (1556), Bishop Manuel de Santo António (1697-1722), and Bishop António de Castro (1740s) and the bishop of Macau, Father José António Medeiros in 1875. Martinho da Costa Lopes, the apostolic administrator for East Timor and his successor, Bishop Carlos Ximenes Belo were post WW II native Church leaders with tremendous impact. Bishop Belo is best known for receiving the Nobel Peace Price (along with current foreign minister, Ramos Horta) in 1996.

Under Lopes and Belo Catholicism firmly became established as the popular majority religion with an over 90% conversion rate. This success however can be as much attributed to their leadership qualities and their tireless efforts in championing the cause of East Timorese against the oppression and brutality of Indonesian occupation both locally and internationally, as to the refuge, protection and spiritual comfort they provided to the population.

After Bishop Belo's resignation the Apostolic Administrator of Dili was Bishop of Baucau, Basílio do Nascimento (since November 26, 2002). In March 2004 the Pope appointed Father Alberto Ricardo da Silva, the former Rector of the Seminary in Dili, as the new Bishop of Dili. Father Belo has served as parish priest in Mozambique since his resignation and has plans to return to East Timor in June 2005 and continue to serve as a priest in the poor countryside (National Catholic Reporter, February 4, 2005)

Animistic beliefs and practices have also been recorded produced by anthropologists in the few existing ethnographies on East Timorese cultures (namely on the Viqueque Tetun, the Marobo Kemak, and the Aileu Mambai). Currently on-going ethnographic work on the Atsabe

Kemak culture also uncovered the strong presence of animistic beliefs and practices that are frequently syncretized with Catholicism. Colonial history makes copious mention of animism in East Timor and a variety of practices were attributed to this belief system, such as those beliefs surrounding the concept of *lulik*(sacred places, objects, and persons).

Sacred places in local cosmology are linked to associations with founding ancestors, the Creator God, and may include specific mountains, forests, rivers, and even caves. Sacred objects tend to be ancestral heirlooms, especially significant objects from oral history of interaction with Sky God, Mother Earth, or battles with the Lord of the Sea. Even heads of enemies taken are sacred due to the spiritual heat of the soul of the deceased; particularly the souls of those who perished in war, accident, or other unnatural death. Ancestral focused rituals are common and the most significant and elaborate for East Timorese are the funerary rites.

Funerary rites are generally expensive due to the number of animals that need be sacrificed or given as part of the gift exchange cycle demanded by obligations of kinship and social relations. Among the Kemak ethnic group, the most elaborate part of the funerary rites are the secondary burials (*leko-cicir lia*, Kemak language) where a number of deceased relatives bones are dug up, cleaned, and reburied, while the soul of the deceased is guided in ritual chants (*nele*, Kemak language) by the clan's sacred man (*gase ubu*, Kemak Language) to the village of the ancestors on Mount Ramelau.

The ritual chants can last over 14 hours as the soul is guided through the origin places of the clan and the places of affinal groups, thus recounting the group's oral history. This ritual has high costs in animal sacrifices, especially that of water buffalo. Other important East Timorese rituals focus on founding houses and their sacred ancestral objects (*lulik*). Such sacred houses (*uma lulik*) have an important role in maintaining traditional social structure and kinship relations. Indeed, after independence a number of such founding houses (*uma lulik*) that were destroyed in the 1999 post-election rampage were being rebuilt with great fervor in spite of the economic expenses of large-scale animal sacrifice.

As a consequence of cultural diversity, there are at least three different styles of sacred houses (*uma lulik*) present in East Timor. The style of *uma lulik* that is a tall pile house is now also a national emblem. Some agricultural rites that focus on the enhancement of fertility of the fields are sometimes still performed but in an attenuated and minimalist manner focusing on planting and harvest only, which local people tend to attribute to a post-colonial attrition and as a consequence of Catholic Church's policies, attitudes, and anti-animistic actions.

However, a late 1960s ethnography on the Kemak suggests that the agricultural cycle rites were performed in their entirety. Rituals tended to be categorized into two types those concerned with life-generation and continuity, and those concerned with death and discontinuity. The specific metaphors and idioms used vary from culture group to culture group. The traditional ritual leaders sometimes coincide with traditional political leaders but nowadays also with Catholic catechists, former war leaders, and current administrative heads.

Atsabe Kemak understanding and attitudes towards what is 'sacred' in Catholicism is informed by and indigenized through local cultural beliefs about *luli* (Kemak). While much of the literature has glossed *lulik* (Tetun) as magic, this is a grievous misinterpretation and mistranslation. Potent spiritual force or power associated with certain places, objects or persons is a more accurate gloss for *luli*. Thus, Kemak Catholics view church buildings, cemeteries and personages and objects associated with these places as sacred.

Thus, clergy are sacred due to the spiritual potency associated with them, much like the traditional sacred men of the clan or village. The cross and statues of various saints, Jesus, and especially of Mary, are also imbued with spiritual potency and thus are *luli*. The Virgin Mary is a special focus of local Catholic veneration. The Mary statue is not only venerated in a similar manner to ancestral objects of *luli* but is given prominence in many village churches in terms of placement, and regular flower and candle offerings. In most rural areas, outside of settlements, one finds grottos carved out of hill or mountain sides beside the road with a Mary statue that is believed to provide protection (much the same way as certain ancestral spirits) for those who seek it while travelling within the territorial boundaries of the village or municipality.

Aspects of local Atsabe Kemak belief and ritual systems: As mentioned above, one of the most important rituals for the indigenous cultures concerns the complex cycle of funerary ceremonies (*tau tana mate*). Funerary ceremonies are the most significant in the Kemak ritual system with large-scale animal sacrifices, and are classified as black rituals, *metama no*. The three main phases of funerary rites include *huku bou, leko-cicir lia,* and *koli nughu.* Brigitte Renard-Clamagirand (1982:143-4), in her ethnography, Marobo: Une Société Ema de Timor, refers to this as *taka no lia* among the Marobo Kemak with several slight variations in the ritual process. According to Elizabeth G. Traube (1986:200), (Cosmology and Social Life: Ritual

Exchange among the Mambai of East Timor), the Mambai also classify funerals as 'black rituals'. Secondary funerary rituals are also present among the Mambai, (*maet-keon*) although there does not seem to be an actual exhumation and reburial of the remains.

Amongst the Atsabe Kemak, *huku bou* is the primary internment of the deceased that requires the sacrifice of at least five buffaloes as well as complementary amounts of goats and pigs. *Leko-cicir lia* is the secondary treatment rite that is the most economically taxing ritual among all rituals of the Atsabe Kemak. Funerary practices are also one of two types of ceremonies that focus on the maintenance of relations with ancestors and on the continuous ritual restructuring of society and the renewal of social relations between the living and the dead as well as between marriage alliance partners.

The *ai mea* wife-giver and wife-taker houses have a central role in large-scale rituals, such as funerary ceremonies, and rituals cannot commence until they all are present. *Ai mea* are the houses that are the original and first wife-giving and wife-taking house to the house(s) that is holding the funerary rites for their deceased member(s). The attendance and participation of all the other *bei-bei* (regular) wife-giving and wife-taking houses is also a strict social requirement. The sacrificial animals provided by the *ai mea* are the animals whose blood is utilized in smearing ritual objects (such as the grave in funerals).

Furthermore, funerals, like all large-scale rituals, must be attended by all the branch houses of the origin house sponsoring the ceremonies (including all the wife-giving and wife-taking house of all the branch houses) as well as those groups/houses that are in a *ka'ara-aliri* (elder-younger) or sibling/friend-ally relationship to the hosting group. Through the death rituals the most important alliances across the generations are confirmed, through the fulfilment of duties via material contributions, exchanges of goods, and the 'blessing' of all the wife-givers of the group whose deceased are honored by such funerary ceremonies.

Indeed the role of wife-givers is part of a larger circulation of sacred power (*luli*) that enhances and contributes to the continuity of life. This circulation also derives from the ancestors and the deceased who will be transformed into ancestors through these rituals. In funerary rituals the contribution of sacrificial animals, in terms of amount and kind of animals, is directly related to the nature of social relationships, and the order of sacrifice itself reflects the hierarchical order of precedence in Atsabe social organization.

As pointed out above, an important characteristic of Atsabe Kemak death rituals is an elaborate secondary treatment of the dead (which in the past also required the taking of heads). This rite is held for a group of deceased relatives (regardless of rank or social status). These secondary rites are especially a grand-scale for local dignitaries, such as a group's sacred men (individuals who are believed to possess concentrated and powerful *luli*, or spiritual potency), the heads of source houses and their family as well as *rati, nai, dato* (lesser chiefs and leaders of the domain), the traditional ritual leaders and *koronel bote* (the ruler of the kingdom). For such prominent figures of power and authority of the kingdom this *leko-cicir lia* ritual is performed for an individual deceased.

The timing of the ceremony is usually before the planting season of dry fields (August-September), thus it is also linked with securing ancestral blessing for the success of the upcoming planting season. This secondary treatment not only concerns the physical remains, but more importantly the soul of the dead that are transformed into ancestors. In the local belief system, if the secondary rites have not yet been performed the soul of the deceased is said to stay near the house and village (*asi naba coa pu*).

The longer the *leko-cicir lia* is delayed, it is believed that the soul of the deceased becomes ever lonelier for companionship, and thus calls the souls of the living to him. So a number of deaths close together in the same family are a sign that the *leko* must be performed and the souls must be transformed into ancestors and transferred to the ancestral villages. This ceremony, however, usually takes place several years after the first interment as it takes a long time to accumulate the economic means demanded by this rite (e.g. for animal sacrifice, cost of feast, grave construction, payment to the sacred man of the group, *gase ubu*, who performs the *Toli* rite, that transforms the soul of the deceased into an ancestor and guides him to the ancestral village).

The closing of the Leko ceremony involves taking the cut-off genitals of all sacrificed animals (the means of creation and procreation) into the depth of the sacred forest, *ai lara hui*, and placing these out of sight at *Bia Mata Ai Pun* (the source of the spring and trees) and asking the ancestors to replenish (return) the animals that were sacrificed in the transferring of the souls of the deceased to the ancestors. This request is performed through a chant while handling the *Loi Ana* sacred beads. In secondary mortuary rites for a ruler, social relations and alliances in an entire kingdom (or now the current administrative units that were part of the former kingdom) become reconfirmed with the fulfilment of ritual obligations and participation

Political activism and role of the Catholic Church in East Timor

The Catholic Church historically had a prominent role in the lives of the East Timorese people. Aside from providing spiritual guidance, they were the defenders of ordinary people against any access or abusive demands placed on them through forced labor by the colonial government and later against human rights abuses by the Indonesian occupiers. The church's strong voice about the plight of the East Timorese people also kept the independence issue in the international arena alive; and Bishop Belo was a co-recipient of the Nobel Peace Prize in 1996. During Portuguese times the Church was also the main educator of the East Timorese—first by the Dominicans and then by the Jesuits. As pointed out in the history section above, many of the current political elite were educated by Jesuit priests.

The Catholic Church, however, also had a strong political interest and role. The historical foundation of the Church's political involvement go back at least to the early 20th century when members of the Church hierarch were formally included in legislative councils under the Salazar government. During the UN transitional administration

(UNTAET and ETTA), prominent priests were also included in the government. Indeed the Catholic Church organized its own civic education programs prior to the Constituent Assembly elections in August 2001. In 2004, while deciding against it, the former bishop, Ximenes Belo, was considering entering politics and running in the next presidential elections.

Given the prominent influence of the Catholic Church on the lives of the East Timorese people, with Catholicism being a major identity marker, the Church has great power in influencing politics. Their influence does not only extend to just through lobbying the governmental powers; but also to organize the masses and influence public opinion. Thus, the Church could easily affect how people might vote or what candidates they might support, as long as they phrase these in terms of following 'Catholic principles'. While the constitution of East Timor separates Church and State and prescribes tolerance and respect for all religions, in the preparatory pre-constitutional phase, the Catholic Church was very heavily lobbying to make Roman Catholicism the official state religion in the constitution.

The prominent political involvement of the Catholic Church is also illustrated by recent events in East Timor. The leaders of the Church, such as Father Domingos Soares, have organized a series of demonstrations and rallies starting on 18 March 2005 that went on for over four weeks. Thousands turned out daily, and it has been reported that the East Timorese police also descended in full force with drawn weapons.

The demonstrations were in protest of a February government proposal to abolish mandatory religious education from state schools and make it voluntary. However, the issues of justice and democracy were also a prominent part of the demonstrations, as the Church wished to express its outrage over the not pursuing trials of Indonesian militia and military personnel who committed atrocities in 1999. The government accused the Church of creating a volatile situation. The church accused the government of being "extremist" and a "dictatorship". The Church also claimed that the people do not trust the government and the demonstrators demanded the resignation of Prime Minister Alkatiri.

It should be pointed out, however, that the Catholic Church representatives were not only pushing for the inclusion of mandatory Catholic religious education in state school curriculum. They also suggested that tenets of other minority religions be also included (such as Islam, Protestantism, and so on). On the other hand, most East Timorese interpreted the Church's outrage on the governmental proposal of excluding religious education as an outrage against not having mandatory Catholic religious education for all Timorese children. It is also interesting to note that some Catholic news sources and in their reports on the situation made certain to point out that East Timor's Prime Minister was Muslim; referring to him as the "Muslim Prime Minister Mari Bin Amude Alkatiri".

By 7 May 2005 the Church and the government reached an agreement with the Prime Minister and bishops of Dili and Baucau, D. Alberto Ricardo da Silva and D. Basilio do Nacimento, signing a joint declaration In spite of a series of preambles referring to parts of the Constitution, the seven point declaration suggests a political victory for the Church in terms of mandatory religious education. It also mandates the establishment of a Permanent Working Group, a month for the signing of the declaration, which will consists of representatives of the Catholic Church and other religious denomination and also government officials to formalize the program of mandatory religious education. The declaration if indeed applied will garner another colossal victory for the Church.

The Draft Penal Code should address the ***abortion*** issue in all its dimensions; abortion must be defined as a crime, except in cases where it is absolutely necessary to avoid the mother's death. The law must equally define the practice of ***prostitution*** as a crime, but should protect victims forced into prostitution.

It would appear that the Catholic Church's activism for legalizing at least some aspects of 'Catholic doctrine and principles' may achieve what they could not prior to the writing of the Constitution -- a Constitutional inclusion of Catholicism as state religion. Should the Church continue with their agenda and succeed, Catholicism might as well have been declared a state religion. It will be interesting to observe the Church's political activities and advances in the next national elections of East Timor.

Language

The lingua franca and national language of East Timor is Tetum, which is a Malayo-Polynesian language influenced by Portuguese, with which it has equal status as an official language. Fataluku, a Papuan language widely used in the eastern part of the country (often more so than Tetum) has official recognition under the constitution, as do other indigenous languages, including: Bekais, Bunak, Dawan, Fataluku, Galoli, Habun, Idalaka, Kawaimina, Kemak, Lovaia, Makalero, Makasai, Mambai, Tokodede and Wetarese.

Under Portuguese rule, all education was through the medium of Portuguese, although it coexisted with Tetum and other languages. Portuguese particularly influenced the dialect of Tetum spoken in the capital, Dili, known as Tetun Prasa, as opposed to the more traditional version spoke in rural areas, known as Tetun Terik. Tetun Prasa is the version more widely used, and is now taught in schools.

The Indonesian language, or Bahasa Indonesia, has ceased to be an official language, although it, along with English, has the status of a 'working language' under the Constitution. It is still widely spoken, particularly among younger people who were educated entirely under the Indonesian system, under which the use of either Portuguese or Tetum were banned.

For many older East Timorese, the Indonesian language has negative connotations with the Suharto regime, but many younger people have expressed suspicion or hostility to the reinstatement of Portuguese, which they see as a 'colonial language' in much the same way that Indonesians saw Dutch. However, whereas the Dutch culture and language had little influence on those of Indonesia, the East Timorese and Portuguese cultures became intertwined, particularly through intermarriage, as did the languages.

Young East Timorese have also felt at a disadvantage by the use of Portuguese, and accuse the country's leaders of favouring people who have only recently returned from overseas. However, even those older East Timorese who do speak Portuguese, having been in the resistance, have not found jobs despite their proficiency in the language.

Many foreign observers, especially from Australia and Southeast Asia have also been critical about the reinstatement of Portuguese. Some of these previously supported of Indonesian rule in East Timor, although others, supported East Timor's right to self-determination. In spite of this, many Australian linguists have been closely involved with the official language policy, including the promotion of Portuguese.

Although Portugal has been closely involved with the teaching of Portuguese in East Timor, there has also been support from Brazil, although there have been complaints from people in East Timor that teachers from Portugal and Brazil are poorly equipped to teach in the country, as they do not know local languages, or understand the local culture.

However, the late Sérgio Vieira de Mello, who headed the United Nations Transitional Administration in East Timor, was a Brazilian who not only established a close working relationship with Xanana Gusmão (now the country's President) as a fellow Portuguese-speaker, but was also respected by many East Timorese because of his efforts to learn Tetum.

Hair removal

Another interesting point of culture is that it is duty for adult women (from the age of 15) in East Timor to remove all body hair (besides their head).

www.ingramcontent.com/pod-product-compliance
Lightning Source LLC
Chambersburg PA
CBHW021114080526
44587CB00010B/517